RAINBOW FARM COOKBOOK

RAINBOW FARM COOKBOOK

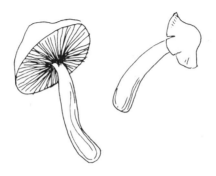

Lynn Andersen

HARPER COLOPHON BOOKS

HARPER & ROW, PUBLISHERS
New York, Evanston, San Francisco, London

Front Cover by Jerry Davis

Text and Drawings by Lynn

Chapter Page Art by Judith Scanlon

Edited and Typed by Rhonda Avidon

Art Assistant - Susan Swift

Book Design and Rear Cover by Allen Gordon

RAINBOW FARM COOKBOOK.
Copyright © 1973 by Lynn Andersen

All rights reserved. Printed in the United States of America. No part of this book may be used or reproduced in any manner without written permission except in the case of brief quotations embodied in critical articles and reviews. For information address Harper & Row Publishers, Inc., 10 East 53rd Street, New York, N.Y. 10022 Published simultaneously in Canada by Fitzhenry & Whiteside Limited, Toronto.

FIRST EDITION: HARPER COLOPHON BOOKS 1973

LIBRARY OF CONGRESS CATALOG CARD NUMBER: 73-5464

STANDARD BOOK NUMBER: 06-090321-x

CONTENTS

*This book is for friends who lived in the attic
and my Rainbow Family,...and thanks for all the
visible and invisible help*

PREFACE

There's a cozy little restaurant in an old
barn-type apartment house, right in the middle
of the town of Woodstock, New York. The tiny,
candle-lit room has been there for about three
years now. The name is the same as its address:
5 Rock City Road. There's no one owner or anything like that. The room has always been run
by a closely-knit interchanging family of young
people. The food is natural and wholesome, and
the prices have always been ridiculously low.
There's no profit-motive...just enough to get by.
Good food, prepared with loving care, and a
peaceful atmosphere. So simple, yet, so hard to
come by.

If any one person set the tone for 5 Rock City,
it was Lynn Andersen. I met her there, about
three years ago. She lived in the back and you
would be pretty sure to find her cooking up some-
thing most of the time. And man can she cook.
I've never seen anyone put so much love and care
into food. Winter or summer, the kitchen was OK
for Lynn.

A couple of years later a bunch of the family
moved out to Phoenicia, which is about thirty
minute drive from Woodstock. That's where
Rainbow Farm began and still is. Over 300 acres
of the most beautiful mountain country...with
a big house, a barn, some goats and ducks too.
The Rainbow Family grew to about 20 folks. Every-
body got into planting and harvesting. Lynn
really got closer to the source of foods. She
learned a whole lot and keptwriting things down.
Soon people started seeking Lynn out and last
year some of her recipes were published in a
national magazine and a cookbook. She asked me
not to mention the names, so I won't, but I did
sneak a couple of lines which I think tell a
whole lot about Lynn, and most certainly apply
to this book.

*"...anyway, that's what I feel this natural
thing is all about...growing, sharing, trading,
and a lot of praying"*.

So, here it finally is...the Rainbow Farm Cookbook. I think you'll find a whole lot in here,
and then some.

Allen Gordon

1
HERBS

SOME TIPS ON HERBS

Cooking and healing with herbs is an ancient art becoming popular once again. Natural living and natural healing go hand in hand. Take advantage of all the healing, soothing, relaxing, energizing qualities of spices, seeds, and green leaves with herbal cooking

Nothing relaxes like chamomile tea, but did you ever think of using it to flavor the salad dressing for your evening meal? Don't feel limited by the word "medicine". These herbs can be used in all your cooking. I find it generally best to use 2 or 3 at the most in a recipe. I prefer the clean single taste of each ingredient that way. I do have some multi-herb and spice curries and "hot countries'" foods. Flowers are not to be forgotten in soups, salads, breads, and puddings.

ANISE SEED

Used in soup, salad, cookies, and breads. It is native to the middle east. Medicinally, it's properties are: relaxant, tonic, carminative, and stomachic. Adds a licorice flavor to food.

BALM (Lemon)

A southern European perennial whose flowers and leaves add a sweet and lemony flavor to soup, stew, salad, and cheese. The plant is used medicinally as a perspiration inducer, carminative, tonic and fever reducer.

SWEET BASIL

An aromatic herb that adds mellow fresh and almost minty flavor to stews, salads, dressings, tomatoes and sauces. Basil is a stimulant, a nervine and is very soothing to the stomach.

BAY

A tree of Rome and southern Europe. Its leaves are used to flavor soup, marinades, and sauces. The herb is soothing to the lungs, throat and nose and also soothing to the bladder or bowels.

SEED POD

ANISE

CARAWAY SEEDS

These seeds are the undisputed rye bread herb.
They are a native to Arabia. Being a biennial,
they are sown at the end of the planting season and they come up, mature and die the following season and must be replanted. The seeds
are used in bread, candy, sauerkraut, sauces,
curries, grains, salads and dressings. The
list is endless. It helps prevent fermentation
in the stomach and aids digestion. It's excellent steeped in hot milk or water 10-20 min.
and given to infants to relieve colic and colds.

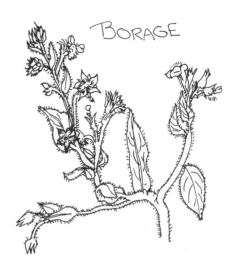

BORAGE

A tasty leaf native to Aleppo. It is used as a
green in tossed salads and as a mild green flavoring in pickles. Even the blue flowers were
used in the claret cups of all European wine
fanciers. Little did they suspect that along
with the warm cheer of the wine, the borage-
claret cleaned the liver and blood of the drink-
er, strengthened his heart and soothed his
throat and respiratory system.

BURDOCK

I have used burdock root as a vegetable, one of
my favorites, and as a tea roasted to make a
coffee-type drink, or raw for a mellow tea or
broth with tamari. It is an excellent herb to
gently cleanse the blood without any strong ex-
pelling of poisons. Great for the kidneys.

CHAMOMILE

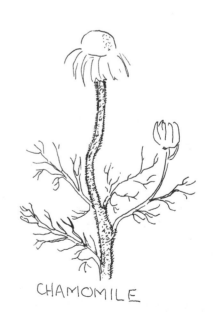

A tiny little petal-less daisy with furry green
little leaves. Besides using it for salads and
dressings, the flowers can be added to breads,
soups, and sauces. It harmonizes well with coriander. Chamomile soothes the stomach and
chest. It's a stimulant, a tonic and also a
relaxant or is mildly sedative. Excellent for
teething children who can't sleep well.

CELERY SEED

A well known pickle lover's herb. It can be used in stews, dressings, bread stuffing, casseroles, and soups. It is a mild tonic, a stimulant and a diuretic.

CHERVIL

A southern European green herb, that can be picked in early spring for light soups, salads, and sauces. I like it especially well with seaweed. This herb is a blood cleanser, aids digestion and is a glandular stimulant.

CHIVES

The little grass that tastes like a mild green onion. They grow easily inside or out and flavor cheese dishes, light soups, salads, and sauces.

COMFREY

The leaves and root are used for any chest troubles or blockages. It is a nutritive plant and aids healing in the body. I've used the young leaves in salad and the root for tea.

CINNAMON

The bark of a tree grown in Malaysia and the area around. Nearly everyone has had cinnamon toast, cinnamon in cereal, in pumpkin or apple pie, cinnamon rolls.

CLOVES

Go well with onion, fruits, beets, and pies. Cloves grow on trees in east India and places of similar climate. One of my favorite smells is cloves stuck in all over an orange and hung as an air sweetener.

CORIANDER

A little round herb seed of the Near East. It is mainly used in breads, soups, sauces and adds

COMFREY: LONG GREEN LEAVES GROW INTO TALL PLANT WITH LITTLE BELL-SHAPED FLOWERS ON TOP.

a mildly sweet and flowery smell to foods. This herb is soothing to the stomach and aids digestion in the lower tract. I've used this in combination with chamomile for a most unusual mild flavoring in soup and sauce.

CUMIN

A seed of the caraway family, its medicinal properties are similar. Cumin seed is my favorite herb for beans and is fine for soups, salads, gravies, and breads. It is one of the main ingredients in curry powder.

CURRY POWDER

A mixture of several spices including turmeric (the yellow substance of curry), ginger, cumin, coriander, cayenne, fennel, cardamon, and various other herbs added for individually flavored curries. Mustard and caraway seeds are two more. Curry is used in soup, sauce, dressing, vegetable and grain dishes, eggs, and pickles. Curry dishes are most pungent and flavorful if the curry powder is roasted a min. or two in a little hot oil before adding other ingredients.

DILL

I don't think I use any herbs more than dill and paprika. The plant is a hardy annual plant which will propigate itself every year from seed. Known best by pickle lovers, it is a multi-use herb for salads, dressings, soups, sauce, vegetables, seaweed, and bread. As a medicine it is a stomach soother, good for colic and gas and also increases breast milk in nursing mothers.

FENNEL

Mainly the seeds are used as flavoring in sauces, soup and I like it especially for breads. The potent little seeds should be used sparingly or the flavor is overpowering. Try sprinkling a few seeds in the bottom of a greased bread pan before adding dough. The entire fen-

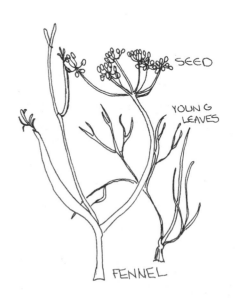

DILL

SEED

YOUNG LEAVES

FENNEL

MINT

PEPPERMINT
STRONG

SPEARMINT
SWEET

MOUNTAIN MINT
MILD

TELL THEM
APART
BY THE
SMELL

ALL
MEMBERS OF
MINT FAMILY
HAVE A SQUARE
STEM

nel plant is used fresh as a vegetable either cooked or raw, and the taste and texture are similar to a sweet celery. Medicinally, fennel dispels gas, calms acid stomach, is a liver and gall bladder cleaner and is even used to allay food poisoning.

FENUGREEK SEEDS

A soothing tea for the throat and lungs, an excellent sprouting seed for salads and sandwiches. Grounded, it is a powdery flavoring for grain and vegetable dishes and excellent in bean soups.

GINGER

Used everywhere in cooking from cake to pickles. It must be used discreetly or it will take over the flavor of anything. Ginger root is healing to the lungs and respiratory system plus being a stomach soother. I find it an excellent tea for breaking up head and chest congestion.

GOLDEN SEAL

Although golden seal is anything but a cooking herb. its strength as a blood purifier, gentle laxative, tonic, an antiseptic and general all round healing properties merit its mention as a tea. It's no treat to drink golden seal. It is truly a medicine and one of the best.

MARJORAM

A little green herb, originally found in North Africa, but probably best known in its use as a flavoring for "Italian foods". It is best when combined with one or 2 other herbs, basil and oregano are an excellent mix for marjoram. Use it in soups, salads, dressings, sauces, stuffing, or herb breads. While you eat, you get your stomach sweetened, your appetite stimulated and your breathing apparatus soothed.

MINT

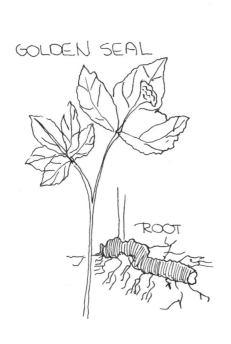

GOLDEN SEAL

ROOT

Soothing, quieting, cooling. Put it in tea,

salads, fruit drinks, and light soups. Some
different types of mint are wintergreen, spearmint, mountain mint, or peppermint. All vary-
ing in flavor from mild and sweet wintergreen
to strong peppermint.

MUSTARD SEED

Used all over the world to spice up vegetables,
sandwiches, sauces. The prepared mustard in a
jar is mustard seed, spices and vinegar, a somewhat weakened version of the hot Chinese mustard
you dip your egg rolls in. The mustard plant
is a delicious salad or cooked green. The
ground seed is well known and used as mustard
plaster applied to relieve aching and congested
areas of the body.

NUTMEG

A plant in the ginger family. The large, hard
seed is grated and used to flavor egg-nog, potatoes, onions, cream sauces, sweet breads,
peas and beans. It prevents food fermentation.

OREGANO

Another little green herb that gives flavor to
spaghetti, pizza and that kind of stuff. Its
uses and medicinal properties are similar to
marjoram.

PAPRIKA

One of the pepper family, a sweet red pepper
originating in Hungary. It is dried and ground
to a red powder to flavor dressings, salads,
sauces, eggs, soups, stews, curries and the
like. It is sprinkled on colorless foods to
brighten them.

PARSLEY

I remember seeing parsley on my plate when I
was little and being told not to eat it, it
was only decoration. It was years later that
I even suspected it was the same plant my moth-
er had dry in jars for cooking. So glad I did.

OREGANO
(WILD MARJORAM)

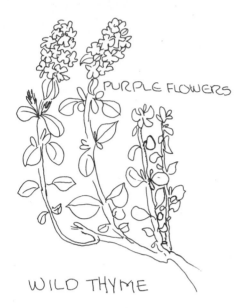

PURPLE FLOWERS

WILD THYME

It is a general flavoring used in most everything and is high in vitamins A, B and C. It stimulates digestion and tones the system.

ROSEMARY

A southern European shrub used to flavor soup, stew, and sauces of Mediterranean cookery. It is a stimulus to the circulatory system and a digestive aid. An excellent herb to rinse the hair or for bathing.

SAFFRON

An expensive little flower of the crocus (bulb) family. It looks like deep orange threads, and just a tiny bit adds sweet, rich flavor and golden color to grains, sauces, vegetables, teas, breads, and noodles. It is usually soaked a few minutes in water before mixing with recipe. It has been known through Biblical times as a spice and fine fabric dye.

SAGE

Well known as a bread stuffing herb for holiday feasts. It's used equally as much as an everyday tea that aids digestion, clears congestion in the respiratory tract, is a throat soother and gargle and is said to strengthen the memory. Use it in cheese dishes, pasta, with onions, and in hot milk, it's delicious.

SAVORY

GARDEN SAGE

In winter and summer it comes from the Mediterranean. Great in bean or pea soups, sauces, cooked dry beans, and potatoes. It is a fermentation preventer and is good for digestion.

TARRAGON

An herb I use less than most, but it has a wonderful flavor when added to eggs, salad, sauces, dressings, and soups. A native of southern Russia and Siberia. I have never run across any medical information on it but I'm sure it has some healing properties. It has a most unusual flavor, a mixture of mild licorice and almost mint.

THYME

Almost a twin of rosemary, they both appear in many Eastern dishes, tomatoes, stews, and dressings. It is used to soothe the nerves and to relieve coughing and other lung troubles.

TURMERIC

The yellow coloring of curry, it is a deep golden root of the ginger family. It's used to flavor dressings, rice, pickles, and relishes. Medcinally, it relieves stiffness in the joints. As a dye it is beautiful, in fact, you can find out how permanent it is if you ever spill it on your clothes.

VANILLA

The spice needed to finish off cakes and puddings, frostings and candy. It originates in the tropics of this hemisphere. The perfect flavoring for sweet foods and drinks. The best flavor comes from boiling the whole vanilla bean in water to extract the flavor. Vanilla extract is commercial flavor that is good, too, but be careful not to get imitation vanilla flavoring which is a cheap, inferior substance.

TARRAGON

SUMMING IT ALL UP!

Of course, there are hundreds of herbs to collect and use. I have explained only the ones used in this book.

A basic thing to know about herbs is the cooking methods. Generally, _leaf_ portions are added for the last 5 to 10 minutes of cooking and as all herbal parts, should never be boiled hard, but only simmered gently or steeped off the flame. In uncooked foods, it is best to have fresh herbs. Allow herb to sit mixed with food so flavor can spread throughout. The

CHICORY

AN EARLY SPRING GREEN SIMILAR LOOKING TO DANDELION GREENS. USE THEM COOKED OR IN SALADS (SOME FOLKS FIND THEM A BIT TOO BITTER RAW). A MOST BEAUTIFUL BLUE FLOWER GROWS UP FROM THESE GREENS.

seeds should be steeped or simmered gently for 10 minutes for tea. For cooking, the flavor is best drawn out of the herb seed by roasting, the heat releases aromatic oils. Roots of herbs are simmered covered 10-15 minutes. For any strong herbal medicine, I like to let herbs steep in water overnight in a cool place.

Herbs are best when they're freshly picked, but few people are lucky enough to enjoy that luxury often. Usually, herbs are only available in dry form. The herb leaf usually is crushed into little flakes. The least crushed form is best. As inner surfaces of the herb are exposed to air, oxidation takes place and nutrients run away into who knows where. If the leaves are stored whole and crushed as used, the flavor, nutritional, and medicinal properties are best preserved. Use air tight jars for herb containers, but make sure herbs are well dried so they don't spoil from moisture. Get roots and seeds whole and crush or grind them fresh. Commercial powdered herbs are the worst. A good deal of the flavor from aromatic oils is dried up and blown away.

In most cases, there should be a light hint of herbs in food. However, I am not one to hold back on spices when I want some real zip-beep in my meals. Again, only you know your own saturation level.

ROOTS CAN BE GATHERED FROM THE YOUNG PLANT AND ROASTED TO BE USED AS A HARDY COFFEE SUBSTITUTE OR MIXED WITH OTHER COFFEE SUBSTITUTES.

BLUE FLOWER

CHICORY

2
SOUPS

ABOUT SOUPS

Anyone who has ever cooked soup knows it will never be the same twice. Here are some basic soups to add to, subtract from or leave the same as you wish.

There are no definite cutting, slicing or chopping instructions. Throughout the soup chapter are illustrations of various ways to cut all vegetables mentioned in the soups. Depending on the appearance you want, you can choose any of the selections of cutting shapes and sizes. The only general rule I follow is keeping the pieces small enough to eat easily with a spoon or chopsticks.

I would like to note here that for any recipe in the soup section, you may use stock interchangeably with water. It is always best to boil the water first then add to soup vegetables. It seals the outer surface and cooks vegetables faster. These are two important factors in retaining utmost nutrients in our cooked foods.

Also in this, as in every other chapter, salt (1/2 t.) may be substituted wherever a recipe calls for tamari (2 T.)

For cooking soup I like a deep heavy enameled cast iron or stainless steel pot with a tight fitting lid. Get a long-handled wooden spoon to stir.

The most important thing about cooking these soups is that you do not feel bound to the recipe, feel free to add or leave off as necessary.

Some nice changes for soups are:

1) Add a handful or two of sprouts after soup is finished cooking. Stir in and cover for 10 min. allowing sprouts to steam before serving

2) Add crackers or broken bits of toast to individual bowls

3) Add pieces of cheese to each bowl before pouring in hot soup

4) I've seen soup served by laying a thin slice of toast in the bottom of a bowl with a slice of cheese on top. Pour hot soup over, toast and cheese float

5) Fresh herbs such as parsley, basil, sage, mint, dill...chopped up and sprinkled on just before serving

6) Grated fresh carrots, cucumbers, green pepper, radish, horseradish...are super additions

Do it!

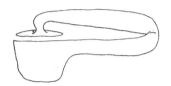

THE USUAL METHOD OF ADDING GARLIC TO FOOD IS WITH A GARLIC PRESS WHICH FORCES THE JUICE FROM A CLOVE OF GARLIC THROUGH LITTLE HOLES AT THE BOTTOM OF A CUP BY CRUSHING IT WITH A FLAT METAL DISC ATTACHED TO THE HANDLE OF THE CUP.

GARLIC BULB

I WOULD RATHER USE THE ENTIRE GARLIC CLOVE.

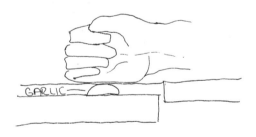

GARLIC

BASIC BROTH (Vegetable Water)

As I chop vegetables, I save the unused parts, carrot and other root tops, skins of onions, hearts of cabbage and lettuce, every unneeded piece not put in a recipe. Store them in a bag or pot until a good bunch accumulates, then put in a pot, cover it well with water. Bring the brew to a boil and slowly bubble 20 min. Turn it off and let it sit there for a couple hours, then drain off the liquid and composte the solid stuff. Use the stock for cooking grains, beans, soups, anything you need liquid for. Add the water left from soaking sprouts, seaweed, everything. It's all got lots of minerals in it. If you can't use all you make for cooking, water your plants with the rest; they like to eat good, too. I used a combination of vegetable broth, seaweed water and herbs that help the growth of plants to water the dirt in our cold trays and they did great.

TO BRING OUT THE ESSENCE OF THE GARLIC OIL, SMASH THE CLOVE UNDER A KNIFE BLADE BY HITTING IT WITH THE HEEL OR SIDE OF YOUR HAND. THEN CHOP OR LEAVE WHOLE -- AS YOU WISH.

LEAFY GREENS

CUT LARGE LEAVES BY ROLLING 2-3 TOGETHER AND CUTTING SLIVERS FROM THE ROLL.

IF PIECES ARE TOO LONG, CUT ONCE OR TWICE ALONG THE LENGTH OF THE ROLL BEFORE SLICING OFF THIN PIECES.

FOR SMALL-LEAFED GREENS, LIKE WATERCRESS AND PARSLEY, TAKE A SMALL BUNCH OF 3-4 STALKS AND CHOP ACROSS IT FROM TOP TO BOTTOM.

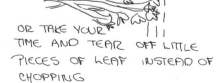

OR TAKE YOUR TIME AND TEAR OFF LITTLE PIECES OF LEAF INSTEAD OF CHOPPING

HEAD GREENS CAN BE QUARTERED OR HALVED AND THIN SLICES TAKEN OFF FOLLOWING THE LINES OF THE PLANT (USE THE GUIDE LINES AS A GUIDE AND CUTTING) AROUND THE CORE.

CLEAR VEGETABLE SOUP #1

2 carrots
2 stalks celery
1 lg. onion
1/2 small head red cabbage
2-3 leaves chard or other green
tamari

Cut carrot, onion, celery and greens into nice-sized shapes for spooning. Shred cabbage. Heat a little oil and add onion, stirring a min.; do the same with carrot for 2-3 min., then toss in other vegetables. Pour in 2 qts. boiling water, simmer 15 min. Add tamari or salt to taste. (for 8)

CLEAR VEGETABLE SOUP #2

2 stalks celery
4-5 sprigs parsley
1 grated carrot
1 bunch scallions
1/2 green pepper
1/2 lb. mushrooms
1 t. fresh grated ginger root
1/2 t. sweet basil
2 cloves garlic
tamari

Bring 3 qts. water to a boil, drop vegetables and herbs in and simmer 5 min. Add tamari or salt to taste. (for 6-8)
This is a light, fresh tasting soup, one of my very favorites.

AUTUMN VEGETABLE SOUP

1 acorn or small butternut squash
1-2 carrots
1 lg. onion
1 sweet potato
1 med. yellow turnip (rutabaga)

Cut vegetables for spooning. Heat a bit of oil in a soup pot and stir-fry onion, then carrots, sweet potato, turnip, squash and cel-ery. Pour 3 qts. boiling water in and simmer for 20 min. Add tamari to taste. (enough for 10)

ONION SOUP

4 med. onions
1/2 t. savory
3 T. tamari
oil

Cut onions in very thin rings. Heat a bit of oil in soup pot and toss in onions, stirring until they are golden and slightly transparent. Add 2 qts. boiling water and simmer 10 min.; add savory and continue cooking 5 min. more. Add tamari and eat like it is or sprinkle with grated cheese. Set a thin slice of toast with a slice of cheese in the bottom of each soup bowl and pour soup over it. (enough soup for 6-8)

DAY LILY SOUP

20 day lily blossoms and unopen flowers
1/4 lb. buckwheat noodles
1 bunch spring onions
3 sprigs parsley
1/4 c. sunflower seeds
8 c. water or stock
2 T. tamari
1 T. oil
1 t. celery seeds

Roast sunflower seeds in pan until brown, add oil and celery seeds, then day lilies, onions and parsley. Add boiling stock, break noodles into it, simmer 10 min. Add tamari and eat.

SPRING SOUP WITH WATERCRESS

big bunch watercress
1 bunch scallions
1 big handful alfalfa sprouts
1 grated carrot
1 clove garlic
8 c. water
1 T. oil
tamari

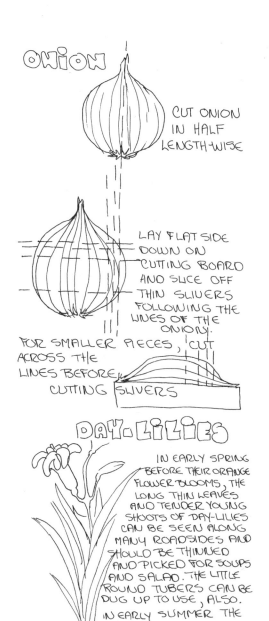

ONION

CUT ONION IN HALF LENGTH-WISE

LAY FLAT SIDE DOWN ON CUTTING BOARD AND SLICE OFF THIN SLIVERS FOLLOWING THE LINES OF THE ONION.

FOR SMALLER PIECES, CUT ACROSS THE LINES BEFORE CUTTING SLIVERS

DAY-LILIES

IN EARLY SPRING BEFORE THEIR ORANGE FLOWER BLOOMS, THE LONG THIN LEAVES AND TENDER YOUNG SHOOTS OF DAY-LILIES CAN BE SEEN ALONG MANY ROADSIDES AND SHOULD BE THINNED AND PICKED FOR SOUPS AND SALAD. THE LITTLE ROUND TUBERS CAN BE DUG UP TO USE, ALSO. IN EARLY SUMMER THE CORAL-ORANGE BUDS APPEAR, OPEN TO BLOOM FOR A DAY AND ARE GONE. PICK THESE SWEET BLOSSOMS AND BUDS FOR SOUP AND SALAD.

WATERCRESS

THIS LITTLE GREEN LEAF CAN BE
SEEN WHEN THE SNOW IS STILL
ON THE GROUND.
IF YOU LOOK HARD YOU CAN
PROBABLY FIND ONE PATCH THAT
WILL LAST FOR MEALS FROM SPRING
TO MID-SUMMER WHEN IT FLOWERS
AND MAKES SEED.
YEAR AFTER YEAR IT WILL REMAIN
IN THE SAME PLACE -- ALWAYS BY
OR IN CLEAR, COLD, AND
RUNNING WATER. THIN
CAREFULLY WHEN CUTTING FROM
A PATCH. NEVER PULL ROOTS
OUT FOR THE PLANT WILL
REGENERATE FROM THEM.

SCALLIONS

SLICE INTO THIN
LITTLE RINGS AND
DON'T FORGET THE
GREEN PART.

Crush and chop garlic, add to heated oil and
saute a couple min. Put in the carrot, stir;
add scallions and watercress, stir a min. Pour
8 c. boiling water to vegetables, simmer 10
min., add tamari and sprouts and serve. (Or:
put sprouts in big bowl on the table and let
everyone help themselves; add mint leaves, just
1 or 2 to the soup. It's good cold.)

WATERCRESS-YOGHURT SOUP

Use "clear" recipe using 1/2 lb. sliced mushrooms instead of carrot and 1 t. salt (no tamari.) Mixing 4 c. water and 4 c. yoghurt, alternate adding them to sauteed vegetables,
stirring until smooth. Eating temperature is
about 100°. If you choose to you can not heat
it and serve it cold by chilling it a bit so
that the yoghurt absorbs the good vegetable
flavors. (serves 6-8)
Either of the watercress soups can be made
with wintercress, a land plant in the same
family. Pick it before it flowers or just when
it has unopened buds. Many people find this
plant bitter once the little yellow flowers are
open. I don't mind the different flavor; in
fact I really like it and don't find it bitter
myself.

HOT CUCUMBER SOUP

2 lg. cucumbers
1 med. onion
2 swiss chard leaves or other green
1 t. basil
tamari

Saute onion a min. or 2 in a little oil. Put
in cucumbers, stir around, and add 1 1/2 qts.
boiling water. Simmer 10 min. Add greens and
basil and cook 5 min. more. Tamari to taste.
(serves 6-8)

COLD CUCUMBER SOUP

2 cucumbers (grate one of cucumbers)
1 med. carrot, grated
1 med. onion
2 stalks celery
4 T. arrowroot flour
tamari

Slice the second cucumber very thin. Saute
onion a min. in oil; add carrot, celery and
cucumbers and stir-fry 1-2 min. Add 1 1/2 qts.
boiling water and arrowroot, dissolved in 1/2
c. cold water. Stir until thick and clear.
Tamari to taste. Refrigerate after cooling
slightly until chilled. (serves 6-8)

CUCUMBER-YOGHURT SOUP

4 cucumbers
1 carrot
1 med. onion
2 cloves garlic
3 c. vegetable stock or water
1 or 2 pinches of cayenne
1 qt. yoghurt
1 T. oil
1 t. salt

Crush the garlic and chop the onion. Saute
lightly in heated oil with cayenne until onion
is golden. Add sliced cucumber (leave the
skins on unless it is a supermarket cucumber
which is usually waxed) and grated carrot, stir
it up. Then add 1 c. of stock and 1 c. of yoghurt, mix smooth. Do the same with all the
stock and liquid adding 1 c. at a time of each
and stirring it smooth. Heat slowly, stirring,
until eating temperature is reached. Add salt
and serve or chill and eat it cold with a
sprinkle of paprika on top. (serves 6-8)

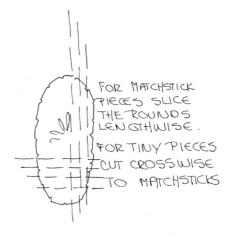

CUCUMBER

RUN A FORK ALONG THE LENGTH OF CUCUMBER TO "SCORE." THIS MAKES THE SKIN EASY TO DIGEST AND IT LOOKS PRETTY.

SLICE ROUND PIECES DIAGONALLY TO EXPOSE AS MUCH SURFACE AS POSSIBLE FOR COOKING.

FOR MATCHSTICK PIECES SLICE THE ROUNDS LENGTHWISE.

FOR TINY PIECES CUT CROSSWISE TO MATCHSTICKS

CURRIED YOGHURT SOUP

Use the above ingredients plus 1 T. curry powder and 3 chopped stalks parsley. Heat the curry powder in the oil for a min. before adding garlic and onion; then follow the rest of the above recipe and eat it with parsley sprinkled on top.

COLD POTATO-CUCUMBER SOUP

2 big potatoes
2 cucumbers
2 stalks parsley
1 bunch scallions or 1 lg. onion
1 qt. yoghurt
3 c. stock
1 clove garlic
2 T. oil
1 t. caraway
tamari

Slice potatoes and cucumbers thin, chop onions, garlic and parsley. Heat oil and add caraway seeds. Saute the potatoes, onion and garlic until potatoes are cooked. Add the parsley, cucumbers and 1 1/2 c. stock. Stir in the yoghurt and the remaining stock. Chill and eat.

CURRY-CARROT SOUP   (for 10 people)

1 lb. carrots
2 stalks celery
1 lg. onion
10 c. water or stock
3 T. sesame seeds
1 T. (round) curry powder
2 T. oil
tamari

Roast sesame seeds until brown and crumbly; add the oil and curry and stir a min. Put in the onion, stir a bit; add the carrot, stir the same and finally the celery. Saute about 5 min. covered. Pour in the stock (boiling) and simmer 10 min. Add tamari and eat.

POTATOES

WHITE OR SWEET CAN BE SLICED INTO THIN ROUNDS AND COOKED

THE ROUNDS CAN BE CUT LENGTHWISE INTO STICKS AND THE MATCHSTICKS CAN BE CUT CROSSWISE FOR BIG OR SMALL CUBES.

MINNESTRONE FOR 12

1 med. zucchini
1 carrot
1 c. cooked chick peas
1 lg. stalk broccoli
4 ripe tomatoes
2 lg. onions
2 stalks celery
1 green pepper
corn from 2 cobs
1/4 lb. green beans
3 cloves garlic
1 t. basil
2 t. oregano
1 T. paprika
oil
salt
tamari

Keep vegetables in separate piles when cutting.
Heat a bit of oil and stir-fry garlic and
onions a min. Add carrot and paprika, stir;
add beans, zucchini, celery, pepper, corn, broccoli, tomatoes and stir together 1-2 min. Next
add chick peas and 4 qts. boiling water, simmer 15 min. Add herbs and cook 5 min. Tamari
to taste.

PUMPKIN SOUP

1 sm. pumpkin
1 lg. onion
oil
tamari

Cut pumpkin into large pieces and steam over
water for 10 min. Remove from heat and cool
enough to peel off skin, then chop into bite-
size pieces. Heat a little oil and saute onion
until golden. Add pumpkin pieces, stir a min.
Then pour in 1 1/2 qts. boiling water (including water from steaming the pumpkin.) Simmer
10 min., add tamari to taste and eat. (enough
for 8)

GREEN BEANS

CUT BEANS DIAGONALLY TO EXPOSE AS MUCH SURFACE AS POSSIBLE TO HEAT OF COOKING. THIS SEALS IN FLAVOR AND NUTRIENTS AND ALLOWS FOR QUICK COOKING.

PUMPKIN

HALVE THE PUMPKIN LAY FLAT SIDE DOWN ON CUTTING BOARD.

SLICE LENGTHWISE FOR BIG PIECES AND THEN CROSSWISE FOR CUBES

POTATO-LEEK SOUP

Follow the potato soup recipe using leeks (2 lg. bunches) instead of onions. Add 2 t. savory leaves with the milk and finish the same way.

CURRY-POTATO SOUP

Use the basic potato soup recipe. Before sauteing the vegetables, heat 1 T. curry powder and 1 T. paprika in the oil for a min. Cook as above and garnish with chopped parsley.

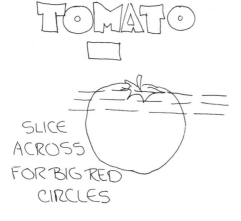

SLICE ACROSS FOR BIG RED CIRCLES

CUT IN HALF AND CUT HALVES IN 3 OR 4 WEDGES

TOMATO SOUP

2 lbs. very ripe juicy tomatoes
5 c. stock
1 lg. onion
1/2 green pepper
2 bay leaves
1/4 t. basil
1 t. oil

Bring stock to boil with herbs and simmer covered 5 min. Chop the pepper and onion. As for the tomatoes: if you have a blender you will puree it with the stock, if you have a food mill, sieve or colander you can mash them through it or maybe you'd rather have the tomatoes in pieces. Anyway you want--saute the onion and pepper in heated oil for 5 min., add the tomatoes and stock and simmer covered 10 min. Put 2 T. tamari in and serve sprinkled with gomasio. (for 8)

CURRIED TOMATO SOUP

Curry tomato soup is made the same way as tomato except you add 1 rounded T. curry powder to the oil before adding pepper and scallions and heating it 2-3 min. Then follow the rest of the tomato soup recipe.

CREAMY TOMATO SOUP

Follow the recipe for creamy mushroom soup
using 6 tomatoes instead of mushrooms and add
a green pepper chopped up. The tomatoes should
be cut in small pieces. During the last few
min. of cooking add 1/4 t. each of basil and
oregano and 2 T. parsley. Then tamari to
taste and eat.

GAZPACHO   (COLD TOMATO SOUP)

4 very ripe tomatoes
1 small onion
1/2 green pepper
2 cucumbers
2 lemons (juice)
1 c. water
2 cloves garlic, crushed
1/4 c. olive oil
2 T. tahini
2 T. tamari
2 T. parsley
1 T. paprika
1 t. basil
1 t. oregano
1/2 t. cayenne

Grate 1/2 the onion, 1/4 of the pepper and 1
cucumber and save. Add all other ingredients
to blender and puree, mixing in large bowl.
Serve with the grated vegetables. For a variation add a pint of yoghurt to blender with vegetables. (for 4)
If you don't have a blender, cut and simmer tomatoes and water together for 15 min. Grate
all the onion, pepper and cucumber and set
aside half of each. Add the other half of
vegetables, garlic, olive oil, and herbs to tomatoes and simmer 5 min. more. Chill well and
beat in lemon juice, tahini, tamari and put
in bowls. Top with other grated vegetables
and serve.

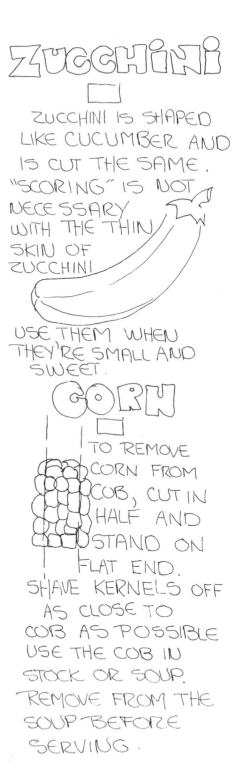

ZUCCHINI

ZUCCHINI IS SHAPED
LIKE CUCUMBER AND
IS CUT THE SAME.
"SCORING" IS NOT
NECESSARY
WITH THE THIN
SKIN OF
ZUCCHINI

USE THEM WHEN
THEY'RE SMALL AND
SWEET.

CORN

TO REMOVE
CORN FROM
COB, CUT IN
HALF AND
STAND ON
FLAT END.
SHAVE KERNELS OFF
AS CLOSE TO
COB AS POSSIBLE
USE THE COB IN
STOCK OR SOUP.
REMOVE FROM THE
SOUP BEFORE
SERVING.

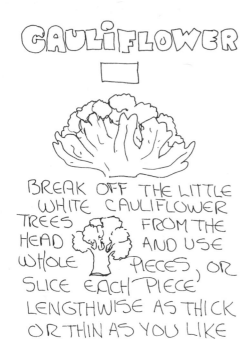

CAULIFLOWER

BREAK OFF THE LITTLE WHITE CAULIFLOWER TREES FROM THE HEAD AND USE WHOLE PIECES, OR SLICE EACH PIECE LENGTHWISE AS THICK OR THIN AS YOU LIKE

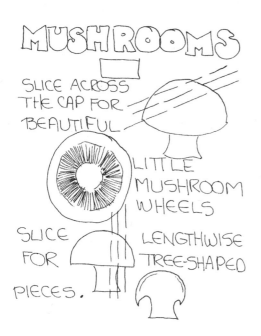

MUSHROOMS

SLICE ACROSS THE CAP FOR BEAUTIFUL LITTLE MUSHROOM WHEELS

SLICE FOR PIECES.

LENGTHWISE TREE-SHAPED

CREAMY CORN SOUP

corn from 6 ears
1 onion
1 sweet red pepper
6 c. stock
1/2 c. whole wheat pastry, barley or rice flour
2 T. oil

Heat oil and add sliced onion, pepper and corn. Saute about 5 min. until onion is tender. Remove to bowl and put flour into pan. Roast, stirring until a nutty smell comes from it; slowly add the boiling stock, stirring the liquid until it's smooth and thickened. Add the sauteed vegetables and simmer 10 min. Tamari to taste. (soup for 6)

CORN TAHINI SOUP

1 1/2 c. cornmeal
2 lg. onions
2 stalks celery
1 c. tahini
2 t. savory
1/2 c. sesame seeds
8 c. water
oil
salt

Roast sesame seeds until brown in soup pot. Add a little oil and saute cut onions and celery, stirring for a min. or 2. Add 6 c. of the water, boiling, bring back up to boil and add cornmeal mixed with 2 c. of cold water. Stir and bring back up to slow boil and cover, simmering 20 min. Turn off and stir in tahini, salt to taste, and serve. Sprinkle with parsley for extra color. (soup for 10)

CREAMY CELERY SOUP

Cut up a bunch of scallions and one bunch of celery, tops and all. Saute in a little oil and follow recipe for creamy corn soup.

TURNIP SOUP

4 turnips (2 purple top and 2 yellow turnips or
    4 purple top turnips)
1 lg. onion
oil
tamari

Heat 2 T. oil and drop in onions, stirring a
min., add turnips and stir 2 or 3 min. Pour in
3 qts. water, boiling, and simmer 15 min., covered. Add tamari to taste and share with 9
friends or family.
Roast 2 T. sesame seeds until brown in soup pot
before adding oil and veggies.
Add a walnut-size lump of miso softened in a
little warm water after soup is finished cooking
and is removed from heat.

TURNIPS CAN BE CUT TO USE AS THIN ROUND SLICES

MAKE THIN MATCHSTICKS BY STACKING A FEW CIRCLES AND SLICING OFF THIN PIECES.

THREE COMMON TURNIPS:
1. PURPLE TOP - - WHITE BOTTOM AND INSIDE

2. RUTABAGA (YELLOW TURNIP) - - BROWN TOP, LIGHT ORANGE BOTTOM AND INSIDE

3. WHITE TURNIP - - LIGHT CREAM COLORED TO WHITE.

THE YOUNG TOPS OF ALL TURNIPS MAKE A - NUMBER 1 GREENS FOR EATING

CREAM OF MUSHROOM SOUP

1 lb. mushrooms
1 onion
1 clove garlic
1 c. tahini
8 c. water or stock
3 T. tamari
oil

Saute garlic and onion until onion is tender,
add sliced mushrooms and stir a min. Put 2 c.
of the water in and slowly add tahini stirring
until smooth. When liquid is hot add remaining
stock and stir again until smooth. Mix 1/2 c.
whole wheat pastry flour with 1/2 c. oil, blend
well and drop pieces into hot mushroom soup,
stirring with wire whisk until thick and smooth.
Add tamari to taste.

MISO

BEST WHEN PIECES OF SOY BEAN HALVES CAN BE FOUND IN THE MISO PASTE. THESE SHOULD BE GROUND SMOOTH BEFORE ADDING TO FOODS.

FOR GRINDING A SURIBACHI (JAPANESE GROOVED BOWL WITH A GRINDING STICK). FOOD IS FORCED SMOOTH AGAINST SIDES OF BOWL.

GRIND WITH A MORTAR AND PESTAL.

OR EVEN A BOWL AND A FORK WORKS GOOD.

BASIC MISO BROTH

Heat 4 c. water to near boiling. Turn off heat and add a ball of miso (about the size of a walnut) which you have softened in a little warm water. Stir and serve.

An analysis of miso shows about 4 grams of protein to 1 c. miso (figuring about 1 healthy t. of miso per c. of water) and is a good mineral supplement helping prevent deficiencies in mineral requirements. Daily replenishment of minerals is necessary to prevent the body from taking them from bones and organs. Some of these minerals are calcium, phosphorous, iron, potassium, magnesium, sulphur, and copper.

Miso contains many bacteria which aid in the digestion of food. If these bacteria are lacking, proper and efficient assimilation of food is interrupted. Never boil miso because it destroys the bacteria, not to mention the flavor of the broth.*

* MISO AND TAMARI, Herman Aihara, Georges Ohsawa Macrobiotic Foundation, Inc., 1972.

MISO VEGETABLE SOUP #1

1 carrot
1 lg. onion
1/2 head green cabbage
1 6" piece of wakame seaweed, washed and soaked
  10-15 min. and cut in pieces
miso, about 4 T.
8 c. boiling water
tamari
oil

Heat oil and add onion a min., carrot and wakame, 2-3 min., and then cabbage 1-2 min., stirring often. Pour in almost all the water (save some to soften miso) and bring to slow boil. Cook 15 min., remove from heat and add miso and a dash or 2 of tamari. (serves 6)

MISO SOUP #2

1 carrot
1 stalk celery
1 onion
1 small zucchini
2-3 leaves chard or spinach
1/2 c. almonds
2 cloves garlic
3 bay leaves
miso
oil
tamari
8 c. boiling water

Saute garlic, onion, carrot, celery and zucchini
in oil. Pour in water and simmer 15 min. Add
bay leaves for last 5 min. Remove from heat
and drop in chard, miso softened in water, almonds and a dash of tamari. (enough for 10)
There is no limit to the combinations of vegetables that can make miso soup. Some harder
to buy but well worth it items are 1) burdock
(absolutely unequaled flavor as far as I'm
concerned): saute a few min. in oil before adding onions and other vegetables using 1-2 thin-
ly sliced roots to the basic miso-vegetable
soup recipes, 2) daikon radish, usually found
in oriental food stores, 3) lotus root, a
large light brown and very beautiful vegetable,
the slices look like little flowers. This
needs to be cooked about 20 min. before adding
other soup vegetables.
Some more common vegetables to combine are:
onion and turnip
broccoli
cauliflower
winter or summer squash
red cabbage
parsnips
kale
collards
scallions
Try adding some fresh grated ginger, chopped
parsley, roasted sesame or sunflower seeds,
herbs or tofu.
You can add almost anything and get fantastic
miso soup.

ACORN:
DARK GREEN
WINTER SQUASH
CUT CIRCLES AND
STACK A FEW TO
CUT JUST LIKE
TURNIPS. OR HALVE FOR
BAKING. ALWAYS COOK
WITH THE SEEDS. LEAVE
WITH THE SQUASH OR
REMOVE FOR ROASTING.
THE SEEDS ARE A
DELICIOUS AND
VITAMIN RICH PART OF
THE PLANT.

BUTTERNUT:
LIGHT CREAMY PINKISH
COLOR. GOOD WINTER
STORER.
CUT LIKE ACORN.

One last thought - I have given amounts of miso to use, but you must decide how strong or mild you like your soup and add or subtract as wanted. Somedays your family needs stronger soup and only you know what days those are.

BUTTERCUP:

DARK GREEN SKIN
WITH LIGHT FLECKS.
LIGHT GREEN BOTTOM.
DEEP ORANGE-GOLD
INSIDE AND SWEETEST
OF ALL SQUASH.

CUT LIKE ACORN.

PATTI PAN:

A WHITE FLAT AND
ROUND SQUASH. LIGHT
TASTE AND TEXTURE.

SIMPLE MISO-NOODLE SOUP

1/4 lb. thin buckwheat spaghetti (or whatever whole grain noodle is available to you)
1 lg. onion
miso (about 3 good T.)
oil
tamari
6 c. boiling water

Heat oil and stir-fry onion slices 1-2 min. Add water, bring to boil, and break noodles into it. Boil gently, covered, for 10 min., just until noodles are tender. Remove from heat and add softened miso and tamari to taste. (6-8 servings)

MISO-NOODLE VEGETABLE SOUP

Follow either miso-vegetable soup recipe, or your own concoction. After adding the boiling water to veggies, bring it back to a boil. Break in noodles and simmer as recipe directs. Then add the miso and serve.
I like to cook my noodles right with the soup because it thickens and enriches the broth. This is true of whole grain noodles only; white, bleached noodles only add starchy glue to soup stock when cooked in it. Also, noodles can be added to any of the vegetable soups without miso, too, and give soups extra substance for those chilly days.

BASIC SPLIT-PEA SOUP

2 c. split peas
1 lg. onion
2 stalks celery
3 cloves garlic
8 c. water
1/4 t. basil
salt or tamari

Bring split peas and water to boil and cook
covered 1 1/2 hours over low heat. While peas
cook, crush and chop garlic, chop onion and
celery. Heat a bit of oil in a pan and lightly
saute the vegetables. Add them to split peas
along with basil and simmer 10 min. together.
Add seasoning to taste. (10 bowls)

SPLIT-PEA TAHINI SOUP

1 c. split peas
1 carrot
1 med. onion
1/2 t. crushed or ground cumin seed
6 c. water
1/4 c. tahini
oil
1 t. salt

Cook split peas and water for 1 hour. Add salt
and cook while you saute cumin seed, onion, and
carrot in the oil, add vegetables to soup and
simmer slowly 20 min. Remove from heat and
beat in tahini. (good for 6-8)

CORN AND SPLIT-PEA SOUP

1 c. split peas
corn from 4 ears
1 stalk celery
2 cloves garlic
6 c. water
salt
tamari
oil

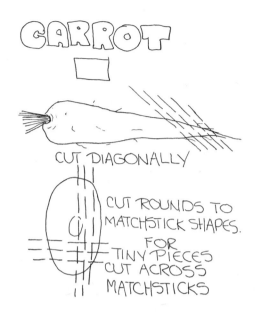

CARROT

CUT DIAGONALLY

CUT ROUNDS TO MATCHSTICK SHAPES. FOR TINY PIECES CUT ACROSS MATCHSTICKS

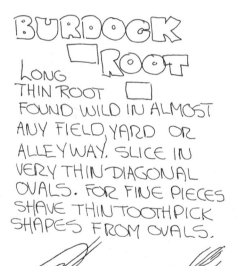

BURDOCK ROOT

LONG THIN ROOT FOUND WILD IN ALMOST ANY FIELD, YARD OR ALLEYWAY. SLICE IN VERY THIN DIAGONAL OVALS. FOR FINE PIECES SHAVE THIN TOOTHPICK SHAPES FROM OVALS.

RADISHES

DAIKON: LARGE WHITE, JAPANESE RADISH. HAS A GOOD BITE. GROWS WELL IN THIS COUNTRY. CUT LIKE A CARROT.

EARLY RADISHES: ARE EITHER ALL RED, ALL WHITE OR HALF AND HALF. CUT AND USE LIKE TURNIPS.

BLACK RADISH (RUSSIAN): ROUND AND ALL BLACK SKIN. WHITE INSIDE. VERY STRONG.

Prepare the peas as you would for split pea soup. Saute garlic, celery and corn for a min. or 2 in oil. Add to split peas when they have cooked 1 1/2 hours and simmer together for 15 min. Add tamari to taste. (6-8 helpings)

ADUKI BEAN SOUP

1 lb. (about 2 c.) aduki beans
1 lg. onion
1/2 butternut squash
2 4" strips wakame seaweed
2 carrots
3 cloves garlic
1 stalk celery
2 T. parsley flakes
oil
tamari

Cook aduki beans for 2 hours in 3 qts. of water with 1 T. oil. Soak wakame for 10 min. and chop it up. Saute with garlic and onion in a little oil for 1-2 min. Add carrot and squash, then celery and saute a bit longer, stirring. When beans have cooked, add veggies and simmer together for 15 min. Add parsley, tamari to taste and eat. (enough soup for 12-16 friends)

BLACK BEAN SOUP

2 c. black beans
2 stalks celery
1 lg. onion
1 t. each of savory, basil and thyme
1 T. caraway seeds

Soak beans overnight in water to cover 3" over beans. Next day add water to bring level 3" over beans again and cook 2 hours with a little oil. Heat 2 T. oil and saute caraway, onion, and celery for 2-3 min. Add to cooked beans and simmer 15 min., toss in herbs for 5 more min., and when done season with tamari to taste. (serves 12)
White or pink beans can be substituted for black beans or a mixture of beans is good and looks beautiful.

SPLIT PEA-WAKAME SOUP

Cook 1 c. split peas in 4 c. water for 1 hour.
Soak a 6" piece of wakame seaweed in 2 c. water
for 15 min. Remove from water and chop into
bite-size pieces. Saute for 2-3 min. in oil
with 2 cloves crushed garlic and 1 lg. onion.
Add to split peas along with wakame soaking
water and simmer 30 min. Tamari to taste.
(6-8 bowls)

CURRIED CARROT-SPLIT PEA SOUP

Follow recipe for basic split pea soup. For
vegetables use 2 carrots, in addition to the
onion, celery and garlic. Heat a bit of oil
and stir in 2 T. curry powder for a min. Saute
the vegetables with garlic and onion first,
then add carrot and cook covered 5 min., add
celery and stir a min. Mix into soup, cover
and simmer 5 min. Add seasoning to taste.

GOOD OLD CHEAP LENTIL SOUP FOR MANY

3 c. lentils
2 big onions
2-3 stalks of celery
2 carrots
4 qts. water
tamari

Bring lentils and water to a boil and simmer
covered 1 hour. Chop up the vegetables and
throw them in the pot or saute them in a little
oil before adding to the lentils. Simmer
covered 15 more min., add tamari to taste and
eat. (enough for a family of 16)

LOTUS ROOT

A ROOT AS BEAUTIFUL AS ITS FLOWER.

THE LOTUS IS A FLOWER CULTIVATED IN THE ORIENT FOR THE ROOT

ROOT GROWS IN SECTIONS AND CAN BE SLICED INTO ROUNDS -- INSIDE THE ROOT IS LIKE A FLOWER. START COOKING BEFORE OTHER VEGETABLES SINCE IT TAKES A MUCH LONGER TIME TO COOK

LOTUS FLOWER

CELERY

CUT
DIAGONAL WEDGES

SLICE STALK ALONG ITS
LENGTH FIRST FOR
SMALLER PIECES.

BROCCOLI

BREAK OFF THE LITTLE
FLOWER SHAPES FROM
THE HEAD AND USE WHOLE
OR SLICE, OR BREAK
INTO SMALLER PIECES.
SLICE THE STALK INTO
ROUNDS OR
MATCHSTICK
SHAPES.

SYRIAN LENTIL SOUP

1 c. syrian (red) lentils
1 onion
1 red pepper (hot)
1 sweet green pepper
2 stalks celery
2 cloves garlic
4 c. water
2 T. curry powder
1 T. paprika
1 t. cumin seed
1 t. oregano
tamari
oil

Bring water to boil and add lentils and a T. of oil. Stir and simmer covered for 45 min. over a low flame. Meanwhile, chop the veggies. Heat 2 T. oil and add the cumin, curry, and paprika, stir for a min. and add garlic, onion, celery, and peppers. Cook covered 5 min. and add with oregano to lentils. Cook together 10 min. Season to taste. (6 servings)

GREEN PEPPER-LENTIL SOUP

2 c. lentils
2 green peppers
1 onion
1 clove garlic
6 c. water or stock
1 T. paprika
2 t. dill weed
tamari
oil

Bring lentils and water to boil and cook covered 1 hour. Chop peppers, onion, and garlic and saute in oil with the paprika for 5 min. Add the vegetables and dill to the lentils, simmer 5 min. Season to taste. (enough for 10)

BULGHUR-CHICK PEA SOUP

1 c. chick peas
1 1/2 c. bulghur wheat
1/2 c. tahini
1/2 c. water
2 t. cumin seed, crushed or ground
3 cloves garlic
1 lg. onion
juice of 2 lemons
3 stalks fresh parsley, chopped
2 T. paprika
tamari
oil

Wash and soak chick peas over night in 12 c.
water. Bring to boil and cook for 2 hours with
1 T. oil (olive oil is good here.) Add bulghur
and cook 30 min. more. Heat 2 T. oil and add
cumin, paprika, garlic, and onion for 2-3 min.
Add to soup and cook 15 more min. Turn off,
heat and stir in tahini, lemon and tamari.
Sprinkle with parsley and serve. (12-16 bowls)

HOT PEPPERS

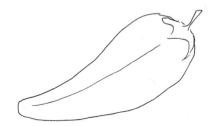

TABASCO:
GREEN WHEN
YOUNG, MATURE
TO RED.

MAKE
BEAUTIFUL
LITTLE ROUND
SLICES

CAYENNE:
SIMILAR TO TABASCO
BUT BIGGER AND FATTER

HOT CHERRY PEPPERS:
LOOK LIKE
LITTLE
TOMATOES

BARLEY VEGETABLE SOUP

To any of the vegetable or bean soups add 1 c.
barley 45 min. before soup is done, and increase
water 5 c. or add 2 c. cooked barley to any
soup and increase water by 2 c.
Other grains can be used as well, such as:
roasted rolled oats, millet, rice or kasha.
Use like barley.

CHEESE AND PARSLEY SOUP

1 lb. white sharp cheddar
1 small bunch parsley
1 c. whole wheat pastry, barley or rice flour
1 bunch scallions
1 sweet red pepper
1/4 c. tahini
1 c. cold water
7 c. water or stock
1 T. oil
2 T. tamari

Heat oil and saute the pepper and onion 5 min.
covered. Meanwhile, mix the 1 c. cold water
with tahini and add to flour slowly stirring it
smooth with a whisk. When vegetables have simmered 5 min. add 4 c. of boiling stock, stir
in the flour mixture whisking smooth. Slowly
add remaining stock, cheese, and parsley and
bring to a boil until thickened. Add tamari
and eat. (it's for 10)
It's all right to leave out the tahini if you
don't have it. Instead, you can add mushrooms
with the pepper and scallions. Put paprika on
it or dill.

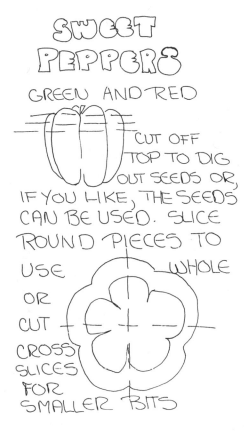

SWEET
PEPPERS
GREEN AND RED

CUT OFF
TOP TO DIG
OUT SEEDS OR,
IF YOU LIKE, THE SEEDS
CAN BE USED. SLICE
ROUND PIECES TO
USE   WHOLE
OR
CUT
CROSS
SLICES
FOR
SMALLER BITS

CARBON STEEL
CUTTING BLADES
STAY SHARP BETTER
THAN ANY. THE KNIFE
BLADE SHOULD BE
THIN FOR CUTTING
VEGETABLES

IT'S A GOOD IDEA TO CHOP
GARLIC AND ONION ON A
SPECIAL BOARD
UNLESS YOU
DON'T MIND THE
TASTE OF THEM IN
ALL YOUR VEGETABLES

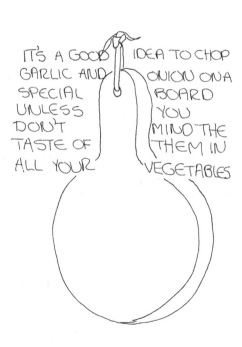

3
SALADS & DRESSINGS

SPROUTS

An easy way to make sprouts is to put alfalfa
seeds (they work great) or other seeds, grains
or beans in a glass jar (one that will fit a
mason jar top.) Cover with cold water and lay
jar on side turning once in a while to move
sprouts around. They do best in a cool place,
about 60-70°, but if your home is pretty warm,
keep them cold by rinsing. After you do it a
couple times, you'll know how often your sprouts
need rinsing. It varies for everyone. You can
have fresh veggies all winter and even summer
if you start a new jar everyday and keep it
going. We have a special shelf up in the kitchen just for sprouts and we do all kinds.

Fenugreek seeds and aduki beans make real
good sprouts, some others are mung beans, lentils, wheat and rye berries, and soy beans. If
you have trouble with soy beans, try crowding
them pretty close in the jar (if you fill the
jar almost to half full, they usually get pretty crowded after soaking.) Beans need more
water than seeds and grains for their first
soaking and need a bit more washing. Sesame seeds and rice make bitter sprouts, but
rice sprouts can be cooked and are really a
good thing. If you put the sprouts by sunlight
you get green shoots. Store them, well drained,
in closed bag or container and keep them loose
(not balled together) while growing and storing.
We eat them everyday in one form or another.

ALFALFA

SOME TIPS ON SALADS

Here's some helpful notes on a few greens that are easy to come by.

Lettuce: There are a number of kinds of lettuce or related greens. They can be used singly, mixed, or with other vegetables. It's best to tear leaves in pieces--easy eating size --rather than cut them, but it's up to you.

Sheep Sorrell: This is a tart little wild green that grows everywhere. It's great alone or mixed with other vegetables in salads.

Purslane: This common garden weed is excellent chopped in salads as well as a good soup or pickling vegetable.

Watercress: Found in or near cold running streams. This is a peppery, but gentle green. It can be mixed or left alone.

CUCUMBER

"SCORE" BY RUNNING A FORK THE LENGTH

MAKES PEEL EASIER TO DIGEST

Here's some things you can add to salads:

Carrots--sliced or grated
Cucumber   "   "
Beets   "   "
Chopped scallions or onions
Sliced raw mushrooms
Raw sweet corn
Nuts or seeds
Broccoli
Cauliflower
Cabbage, red or green
Raw green beans
Radishes
Peppers
Sprouts

ICEBERG (HEAD)LETTUCE

ROMAINE LETTUCE

TALL HEAD

BOSTON AND BIBB LETTUCE BOTH HAVE SMALL LOOSELY-PACKED HEAD LETTUCE

OAK-LEAF LETTUCE LEAVES GROW IN BEAUTIFUL CLUSTERS

CHICKORY DARK GREEN LEAVES

AVOCADO SALAD #1

1 well ripened avocado
1/2 c. tahini
juice of 2 lemons
1/2 t. ground cumin seed
1 small bunch scallions
2 cloves garlic, crushed and chopped
2 T. tamari

Mix tahini and other ingredients and let sit
while you mash the avocado. Then mix it all
together. (makes about 1 1/2 cups)

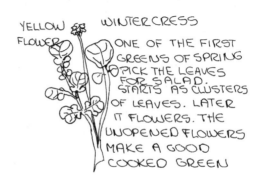

YELLOW
FLOWER

WINTERCRESS
ONE OF THE FIRST
GREENS OF SPRING
PICK THE LEAVES
FOR SALAD.
STARTS AS CLUSTERS
OF LEAVES. LATER
IT FLOWERS. THE
UNOPENED FLOWERS
MAKE A GOOD
COOKED GREEN

LAMB'S QUARTERS

COMMON WILD EDIBLE --
DELICIOUS IN SALAD.
LEAVES HAVE A LILAC-
COLORED DUST ALL OVER
THEIR BASE.

AVOCADO SALAD #2

8 oz. or 9 oz. of cream cheese
1 well ripened avocado
2 cloves garlic, crushed and chopped
juice of 2 lemons
1 t. salt
1 T. paprika
2 T. dry parsley or 2 sprigs fresh
1/4 t. cayenne
2 T. olive oil

Soften cream cheese and beat smooth with lemon
and seasoning. Let it sit and mash avocado with
garlic and oil. Add to cream cheese, mixing
until smooth. This is good to stuff in or
spread on anything. (makes about 2 cups)

SPINACH MUSHROOM SALAD

Take 2-3 nice bunches of fresh spinach, (the fresher the better). Break into pieces...save stems and chop them like celery. Slice 1/2 lb. white mushrooms and 1 bunch scallions into thin slices and toss together with spinach.
This salad is great with yoghurt, bleu cheese dressing, or lemon and oil. All dressings taste fine, so you must decide what you like best by trying different combinations.

COLESLAW   (CABBAGE SALAD)

1 lg. head cabbage, green or red and green, shredded
3 carrots, grated
1 green pepper, finely chopped
1 med. onion or, 1 bunch scallions

Mix above with 1 t. salt and 1 c. soy mayonnaise and juice of 2 lemons.
For tart-tart salads use vinegar and oil dressing. Dill is good, too.

CUCUMBER AND BASIL SALAD

Score 4 cucumbers and chop into bite size pieces. Toss 2 t. basil and let sit together 10-15 min. Mix again and serve. (for 6)
Great with yoghurt dressing or vinegar and oil.
Dilled cucumber is done the same way, but add dill weed instead of basil.

GREEN BEAN SALAD

Steam 1 lb. green beans over water for 5 min. Chill and marinate in a dressing of juice from 2 lemons, 1/2 c. oil, 1/4 c. water, 2 chopped cloves of garlic, and 1 t. salt mixed together. Add 1 bunch scallions to chilled beans. Mix with marinade and sit together 10-15 min.

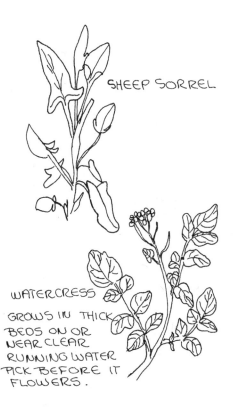

SHEEP SORREL

WATERCRESS
GROWS IN THICK BEDS ON OR NEAR CLEAR RUNNING WATER PICK BEFORE IT FLOWERS.

TEAR SALAD GREENS INTO
BITE-SIZE PIECES. RATHER
THAN CUT.

PURSLANE
A COMMON GARDEN
WEED -- GROWS LOW
TO THE GROUND AND
BRANCHES OUT LIKE
A VINE. STEM IS
DARK RED. GOOD
SALAD GREEN.

STUFFED TOMATO SALAD

Cut a hole into tops of 4 good sized tomatoes.
Fill with a mixture of 1 soft avocado-mashed,
2 or 3 chopped scallions, juice of 1 lemon, 1/2
t. salt, 1 crushed clove of garlic, and 2 t. oil.

TOMATO-ONION-CUCUMBER-YOGHURT SALAD

Chop 4 tomatoes into eating pieces. Slice 1 big
bunch of scallions or 3 little onions into rings.
Score 2-3 cucumbers and cut in pieces. Mix with
1 t. salt and 1 qt. yoghurt. (serves 6)

POTATO SALAD

Boil 2 lbs. potatoes until soft. Chop 3 stalks
celery, 2 med. onions, and grate 2 carrots.
Drain potatoes and chop up, with skins. Mix
with other vegetables, 2 t. salt and 2 c. soy
mayonnaise (or regular). Sprinkle with paprika
and allow to sit together a few min. Eat at
room temperature or chill in frig. (serves 4-6)

SWEET POTATO SALAD

Done the same as regular potato salad.
Both potato salads may have 4-6 chopped hard-
boiled eggs if richer taste is desired.

JERUSALEM ARTICHOKE SALAD

Wash and cook 2 lbs. jerusalem artichokes in
water until soft. (Boil, then simmer). Drain,
saving water for soup stock. Cut into bite-
sized pieces. Chop 1 bunch scallions, 3 stalks
celery, 1 green pepper, and 1 scored cucumber.
Grate 2 carrots and mix with artichokes. Mix
together: 1 c. oil, 1/2 c. water, 1 t. salt,
juice of 2 lemons, 2 crushed cloves garlic, 1 t.
dill. Pour over artichokes and vegetables.
(serves 6-8)

MARINATED BEETS AND HORSERADISH

Take 2 lbs. beets, slice in rounds and steam 10 min. over water. Put in a bowl and sprinkle the top with 2 round t. of grated horseradish. Mix together 1 c. cider vinegar, 1 c. water, 1/4 c. honey, 1/4 t. cinnamon, 1/4 t. allspice, in a pan. Heat until steaming and honey is dissolved. Pour over beets. Allow contents to chill at least 2 hours or overnight.

BULGHUR-PARSLEY SALAD

3 c. cooked bulghur (wheat pilaf)
1 lg. bunch fresh parsley or 1/2 c. dry
3 cloves garlic, chopped
2 T. tahini
1/3 c. olive oil
1 t. salt
juice of 2 lemons
2 T. paprika
1/4 t. fresh ground cumin seed

Mix together bulghur and parsley. Add dressing to it made from remaining ingredients. Let mixture sit together a bit.   (serves 4)

CABBAGE
GREEN AND RED

CUT BY QUARTERING AND SHREDDING THIN SLICES OFF FOLLOWING THE LINES OF THE CABBAGE LEAVES AS A GUIDE.

MUSHROOMS

SLICE THROUGH CAP FROM TOP TO BOTTOM. SOMETIMES I LEAVE STEM ON AND SOMETIMES I SLICE IT SEPARATELY.

FOR ROUND PIECES AND LARGE MUSHROOMS CUT ACROSS TOP OF CAP.

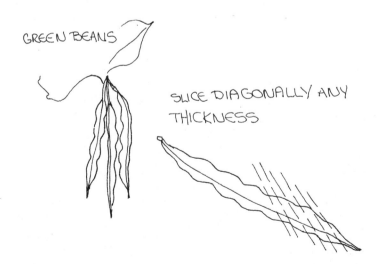

GREEN BEANS

SLICE DIAGONALLY ANY THICKNESS

TOMATO STUFFING
CUT A CROSS IN THE
TOP OF THE TOMATO
AND SPREAD FOUR SECTIONS
APART. SCOOP A LITTLE
OF THE TOMATO OUT AND
ADD TO FILLING OR STUFF
AS IS.

AVOCADO

DARK GREEN (AND OFTEN
BUMPY) SKIN AND
YELLOW-GREEN INSIDE.
MUST BE VERY SOFT TO
SQUEEZE BEFORE EATING.
LEAVE AT ROOM TEMPER-
ATURE TO RIPEN.

PEEL OFF OUTER
SKIN, REMOVE PIT
AND SLICE FOR
SALADS AND IN
COOKING OR FILL HALVES
WITH STUFFING OR SALAD.

AVOCADO FRUIT SALAD

2 avocados, soft-ripe
juice of 2 lemons
2 cloves finely chopped garlic
1 lg. tomato
1/2 sweet red pepper, finely chopped
1 sm. onion, finely chopped
1/4 t. cayenne
2 t. olive oil
1 t. salt

Mash up avocados into a smooth paste. Add tomato, onion and pepper. Mix together the garlic, oil, lemon, salt and cayenne and pour into avocado. Mix well. (lunch for 4)
Or:
Serve on a bed of lettuce and alfalfa sprouts,
(probably enough for 6)
Or, mix with 8 oz. softened cream cheese and
use as a spread for bread.

APPLE-RAISIN-NUT SALAD

6 big apples
1 c. chopped mixed nuts (or your favorite kind)
1/2 lb. or 1 c. raisins
2 lemons for juice
1 c. soy butter
3 T. honey

Slice apples (skins, too). Mix everything together with a pinch of salt. Let it sit a few
min. and eat. (serves 4-6)
Other things to do with this basic salad is to
make:

CELERY-APPLE-NUT by adding 3 stalks of chopped
celery.
BANANA-APPLE-NUT by mixing in 3 very ripe bananas, sliced.
YOGHURT-APPLE by adding 1 pt. yoghurt instead
of soy butter and increasing the honey to 4 T.
Serve with just lemon and honey.

CANTELOUPE-DATE SALAD

1 well ripened canteloupe
1 sm. head cauliflower
1 bunch scallions
1/2 lb. dates

Take out seeds and peel canteloupe. Cut into
bite-size pieces. Pit and chop dates. Break
cauliflower into little flowers and slice scallions in rings. Toss together with 1/4 c. vinegar, 1/4 c. water, 1/2 c. oil, 3 T. honey,
and 1 t. salt

PEACH-ALMOND SALAD

2 lbs. fresh peaches
3 stalks celery
1/2 lb. almonds
4 T. honey
1 pt. yoghurt
1/4 t. cinnamon
juice of 1 lemon
pinch of ground coriander

Mix together yoghurt, honey and spices and set
aside. Chop the almonds and celery and slice
the peaches. Mix it all together and serve.
(salad for 4-6)

PINEAPPLE-NUT SALAD

1 ripe pineapple
1/2 lb. dates
1/4 c. honey
1/2 lb. mixed nuts, such as walnuts, cashews,
 pignolias, pecans, etc.
1/2 lb. dark cherries

Cut the pineapple chunks to eating size. Chop
the nuts and dates. Halve and pit cherries.
Mix together with lemon and honey. (serves 4)

MELONS

BEST EATEN
ALONE OR WITH
OTHER MELONS

WATER MELON
USUALLY WELL-RIPENED
IF HOLLOW SOUNDING
WHEN THUMPED WITH A
FINGER. SHAPES VARY
FROM ROUND TO OBLONG.
DARK GREEN TO LIGHT
SKIN.

HONEYDEW
LIGHT GREEN, ROUND
GOOD WITH FRESH LEMON
SQUEEZED ON IT.

CANTELOUPE
LIGHT TAN SKIN
WITH BUMPS. SMALLER
THAN THE OTHER
MELONS.

STRAWBERRY-PEACH FRUIT KANTEN (Agar-Agar)

1 pt. strawberries
3-4 peaches
1/4 c. tahini
2 c. cold water
1 qt. apple juice
1/2 c. honey
2 sticks agar-agar (kanten)

Soak agar-agar in cold water for 15 min. Bring
to boil and boil slowly for 10 min. until the
kanten has dissolved. Add apple juice and honey. Stir and let sit until cool. Slice clean
strawberries in half. Slice peaches thin. Add
to the agar-agar mixture along with tahini.
Pour into a dish to set. Refrigerate until
thickened. (serves 8)

PEAR SALAD

6-8 ripe pears
1/2 lb. dry currants
3 T. honey
2-3 fresh mint leaves, or 1-2 dry leaves
1/4 c. oil
1/2 t. cinnamon
1/2 lb. chopped pumpkin or sunflower seeds
juice of 2 lemons
1/4 c. oil

Mix honey, lemon, oil, water, cinnamon, and mint
leaves together. Pour over currants in a lg.
mixing bowl. Cut up pears for eating (with
skins) and mix along with pumpkin seeds into
currants. (6 portions)
Of course, you can also use yoghurt in this
salad.

BANANA

PINEAPPLE

CUT OFF TOP AND
BOTTOM, AND ROUGH OUTER
SKIN. REMOVE CORE AND
SLICE RINGS.

OR QUARTER PEELED,
WHOLE FRUIT AND SLICE
CORE FROM THE
WEDGES AND
CUT INTO
TRIANGLES.

BANANA-NUT SALAD

3-4 well ripened bananas
1 soft avocado
1 fresh coconut, grated or 2 c. shreds
2 c. yoghurt
1/4 c. honey
1/4 t. ground allspice
2 lemons, for juice

Mix together honey, allspice, coconut shreds
and yoghurt. Peel and slice bananas and avocado. Add lemon juice. Add yoghurt mix.
(serves 6-8)

KANTEN
(AGAR-AGAR)
WHITE, TRANSLUCENT
SEAWEED
COMES IN 1/4-OUNCE
STICKS AND IS USED
AS A GELLING AGENT IN
MOLDED SALADS AND
DESSERTS.

APPLE-RAISIN-NUT KANTEN

4-5 sweet apples
1/2 lb. raisins
1 c. chopped assorted nuts
2 sticks agar-agar

Soak and cook agar-agar as in strawberry-peach
recipe (above). Add raisins, apples, and nuts
while mixture is hot. Pour into dish to set in
refrigerator. (plenty for 6)

STRAWBERRY

APRICOT-COCONUT KANTEN

1/2 lb. dry unsulphured apricots
1 qt. apple juice
1 c. shredded coconut or 1/2 fresh grated coconut
2 sticks agar-agar
2 c. water

Fix agar-agar and water as in other kanten recipes. Soak apricots and dry coconut in apple juice. When agar-agar has boiled 10 min.,
remove from heat and add apricots and coconut.
Refrigerate until firm. (6 portions)

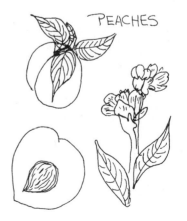

PEACHES

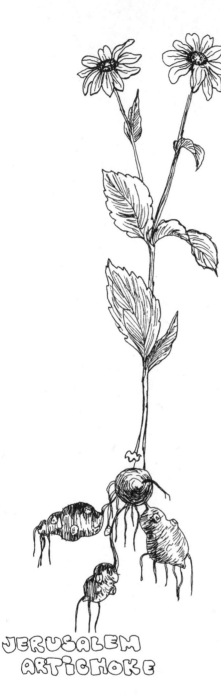

JERUSALEM ARTICHOKE

TAHINI-LEMON-HERB

1/2 c. oil
juice of 2 lemons
1/4 t. chervil or basil
2 T. dry parsley or 3 stalks fresh
1/2 c. water
4 T. tahini
1 T. paprika
2 T. tamari or 1 t. salt
1 gib clove garlic

Follow one of basic recipes for mixing ingredients. Using the basic methods of mixing, try these combinations:

LEMON AND OIL   (Basic)

1/2 c. oil
1/3 c. water
juice of 2 lemons
1 t. salt

With Herbs: To the basic dressing add 1/4 t. each, oregano and basil, 1 clove garlic, and 2 T. dry parsley or 3 stalks fresh.

With Tomato: Add 1/2 c. pureed tomatoes to either basic dressing or herb.

With Cheese: Crumple bleu cheese, feta, grated hard cheese into any of the above lemon-oil dressings. (1 1/2 cups)

With Yoghurt: To any of the above recipes, beat in 1/2 pt. yoghurt. (2 cups) Sour cream is good, too. Even sweet cream is nice.

LEMON AND OIL   (Basic)

juice of 2 lemons
1/3 c. water
1 clove garlic, chopped
2/3 c. oil
1 t. salt

Shake it together and pour on salad. (little over a cup)

With Herbs: Add 1/4 t. basil, oregano, 1 T.
dill weed, paprika or any other herbs you
like. Parsley, chives, etc.

With Tomato: Mash tomato up well and add to
either of the above 2 dressings, shake it up.

With Cheese: Add 1/2 lb. crumbled blue, stilton,
gorgonzola, roquefort or grated hard cheese,
or feta.

With Sour Cream or Yoghurt: Add any lemon
and oil dressing slowly to 1/2 pt. sour cream
or yoghurt.

With Vinegar and Oil: Substituting 1/4 c. vinegar for lemon juice, make lemon and oil
dressings.

SOY BUTTER DRESSING

This is made almost the same as soy butter for
spread, only it'll be thinner.

2 c. oil
2 c. water
2 lemons
3 T. soy flour

If you have a blender, heat flour and water.
Boil gently 5 min., stirring a bit. Pour liquid into blender and turn on, adding oil in a
slow, steady stream until thick and creamy, and
oil is gone. Add lemon and salt to taste.
(makes 1 quart)

With Garlic: 2 cloves of garlic is great to
add. Just crush and chop fine.

With Herbs, Plants, and Spices: There are so
many good ones. Try 2 T. dill weed, 2 t. caraway seeds, 2 T. paprika, 1/2 t. mustard seeds
freshly crushed, 1/2 t. cayenne, 2 T. curry
powder (heated with the flour and water), 2 T.
grated horseradish.

THE JERUSALEM ARTICHOKE IS NEITHER FROM JERUSALEM, NOR IS IT AN ARTICHOKE THE PLANT IS NATIVE TO NORTH AMERICA, FOUND IN LOOSE, MOIST SOIL. THE FLOWER LOOKS LIKE A MINIATURE SUNFLOWER AND BLOOMS IN THE FALL. THE TUBERS ARE READY FOR EATING WHEN THE FLOWERS STOP BLOOMING AND MAY BE PICKED FOR EATING THEN OR DUG UP IN SPRING.

PERFECT POTATO SUBSTITUTE IN SALAD WITH EGGLESS MAYONNAISE

GRAPES

FRUIT GROWS ON THICK VINES. YOUNG LEAVES CAN BE EATEN AS A GREEN OR STUFFED LIKE CABBAGE LEAVES.

TWO COMMON GRAPES:

GREEN SEEDLESS
  SMALL, LIGHT GREEN
GOOD EATING AND IN SALADS

CONCORD
  DARK PURPLE WITH LITTLE SEEDS—EAT THE SEEDS IF YOU CAN OR SAVE FOR JELLY MAKING FOR COOKING IN BREADS.

CONCORD GRAPES

GRAPE CUSTARD KANTEN

1 qt. dark grape juice
1 qt. plain yoghurt
1/2 lb. green grapes
2 sticks agar-agar
1/2 lb. sunflower seeds
1/2 c. water
1/4 c. honey

Soak and cook agar-agar and water as other recipes. Wash and remove grapes from stem. When kanten has finished cooking, remove from heat and add honey, grapes, and seeds. Stir well and cool, then beat in cold yoghurt. (serves 8)

BLUEBERRY-LEMON KANTEN

1 pt. fresh blueberries
juice of 6 lemons
1/2 c. honey
1/4 c. tahini
2 sticks agar-agar

Soak agar-agar in water and cook as in other recipes. When done, turn off heat and add blueberries, honey, and lemon juice. Mix well. Beat in honey. Cool until firm. (for 6)

DRESSINGS

EGGLESS MAYONNAISE

2 c. oil (light)
juice of 1 lemon
cayenne
salt
1 c. water
2 round T. soy flour

Make the same as soy butter. After adding oil and lemon, salt and a pinch or two of cayenne.

PICKLE AND TOMATO DRESSING

To soy-garlic dressing add:

2 T. paprika
2 ripe tomatoes, chopped
1 t. salt
1/4 chopped sweet pepper
1/3 c. chopped sweet pickles

CUCUMBER-YOGHURT DRESSING

1 med. cucumber
1/2 pt. yoghurt
2 cloves garlic, chopped
1/2 c. oil
1/2 c. water
1 T. tamari
1/2 t. salt
juice of 1 lemon
1 t. paprika
2 t. caraway seeds

Score and chop cucumber. Mix water and oil into yoghurt. Add lemon, garlic, tamari, caraway, paprika, and salt. Stir well and let sit 20-30 min. Stir again and serve. This is great on a salad of spinach and raw sliced mushrooms.

YOGHURT-HERB DRESSING

Make above dressing with or without cucumbers and add 1 T. dill weed or add any herb you like.

HONEY-YOGHURT

Sweeten yoghurt with honey to taste and use on fresh or dry fruit salads. Add some spice, coriander, cinnamon, allspice.

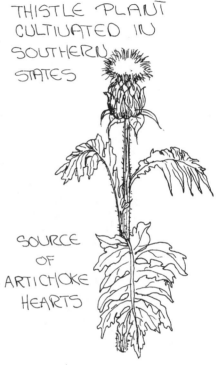

GLOBE ARTICHOKE

THISTLE PLANT CULTIVATED IN SOUTHERN STATES

SOURCE OF ARTICHOKE HEARTS

STEAM WHOLE ARTICHOKE FOR 20-25 MIN. AND EAT WITH MUSTARD SEED SOY BUTTER BY DIPPING SOFT END OF LEAVES IN AND ENJOYING.

4
FRUITS & VEGETABLES

APPLE SAUCE #1

1 1/2 lbs. apples
8 oz. water

Puree apples raw with skins and seeds in 8 oz.
water. Serve right away. (makes 3 1/2 - 4 c.)
Or: Heat to 185°, pack in sterile 1/2 pint
jars, seal and process 20 min. in boiling bath.

APPLE SAUCE #2

3 lbs. apples
8 oz. water

Drop sliced apples into boiling water, cover
and bubble 10 min. Put through a sieve, colander, or food mill to puree. Serve warm, cold,
with cinnamon, allspice, coriander, mint.
(about 6 cups)
Heat to 185°, pack in sterile jars, seal and
process 20 min. in boiling water.
Every food is canned a little differently. Most
mason type jars have cooking and processing
times inside the cartons but if not, you can
get a nice canning book for 35¢ from Ball or
Kerr mason jar manufacturers.

APPLE BUTTER

5 lbs. apples
a bit of water, not more than a c.

Cut apples, seeds, skins and all, and cook over
med.-high flame in covered stainless or enamel
pot with water. (Iron discolors apples and
leaves a metallic taste). Cook apples until
very soft. Puree through sieve, food mill, or
in blender. When apples are pureed, return to
a cooking pan and set on a low flame in a pan
of water. Allow to cook covered 4-6 hours, until thick and dark. Put in sterile jars, seal
and process 20 min. in boiling water or eat
immediately.
(makes about 4 pints apple butter)

APPLE-TAHINI WHIP

Cook a pound of apples until soft, then puree.
Mix with 1 c. tahini and eat on bread or crackers. (makes 2 1/2 cups)

BAKED APPLES

Apples can be baked whole, cored, sprinkled with
cinnamon, stuffed with raisins and nuts, basted
with maple syrup or wrapped in a ball in pie
dough and baked at 375° for 30 min.

APPLE-APRICOT SAUCE

1/4 lb. dry apricots, soaked several hours in
   3 c. water

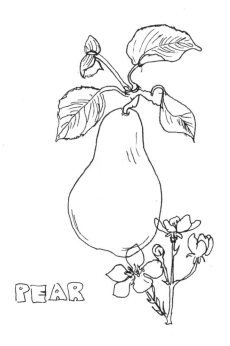

PEAR

Cut up and puree in blender with the remaining
water and 1 1/2 lbs. apples with skins and seeds.
Or: Heat apples, apricots and water until
fruits are just tender enough to put through
a sieve or food mill.
Heat mixture to 185° and jar immediately in
sterile pts. or 1/2 pts. Process 10 min. at
10 lbs. pressure or 20 min. in boiling water
bath.
Or: Eat it right away on bread, crackers,
fruit salad, in yoghurt.
Or: Cook until thick and dark before jarring
or eating. Do this like apple butter. Add
spices.

APPLE-PRUNE SAUCE

Add 1/2 lb. soaked pitted prunes to apple butter or apple-apricot recipe. A touch of mint
in the cooking water is really nice. Juice
from a lemon or 2 is fine.

STEWED PRUNES

Put prunes in saucepan covered with boiling
water. Let soak over night. Stir and heat,
covered, over low heat until just eating temperature. Serve. 1 lb. prunes makes about
4 c. stewed prunes.
If you're serving children, it's a good idea
to pit the prunes before heating.
Try squeezing lemon on top. Yoghurt in or on,
also.

SPICED PRUNE WHIP

Add 1 T. cinnamon, ground or 2 sticks, 1 t. allspice, 1/4 t. coriander and 1 T. grated lemon
peel to prunes along with boiling water.

MIXED FRUIT COMPOTE #1

1/2 lb. raisins
1/2 lb. dry unsulphured apricots
1/4 lb. dry currants
1 lb. prunes
1/2 lb. honey dipped, dry pineapple

Pour 3 qts. boiling water over this and allow
to sit over night. Bring slowly to eating
temperature and eat. Same things are true of
this as stewed prunes.

MIXED FRUIT COMPOTE #2

1 lb. fresh peaches
1/2 pt. fresh blueberries
bananas (2-3)
1 pt. strawberries
1 lb. green grapes

Mix together after cutting in eating size pieces. Use with the same things as stewed prunes.
(serves 8 folks)
Sour cream is great on this.

SWEET CHERRY

CANTELOUPE-HONEYDEW-LEMON

Cut, seed and peel 2 ripe canteloupe and 1 honeydew. Cut in bite size pieces and mix with the
juice of 2 lemons. Eat immediately and by itself to get the most out of it.
(enough for 4-6)

APRICOT-MINT STEW

1 lb. dry unsulphured apricots
1 1/2 qts. boiling water
2-3 sprigs of fresh mint or 3-4 T. dry mint

Pour 2 c. boiling water over mint leaves. Let
steep covered for 30 min. Pour 1 qt. of water
on apricots and soak 2-3 hours. Add mint and
serve. Good with yoghurt on top.

GINGER-PEARS

Slice 2 lbs. of pears in very thin slices and
mix with the juice of 4 lemons. Chill. Bring
to a boil 1/2 c. water, 1/4 c. honey and 2 T.
fresh grated ginger or 4 slices of root, or
2 t. dry ground, if you have to. Boil gently
10 min., cool a bit and pour over pears just
before eating. This isn't bad with yoghurt,
either.

BANANAS BAKED IN THE SKINS

Bake 20 min. in 350° oven or until skins split.
Remove and baste with lemon and honey.

THE BANANA IS
NOT A TREE
BUT A
PERENNIAL
HERB.

BANANA

FRIED BANANAS

Peel bananas, cut in half crosswise and slice
thin lengthwise pieces. Dip in lemon or orange
juice and coat with a light flour. Saute until
golden in shallow or deep oil.

STEAMING

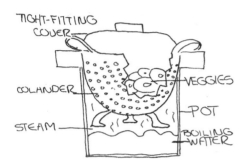

TIGHT-FITTING COVER

COLANDER

STEAM

VEGGIES

POT

BOILING WATER

A COLANDER OR SIEVE MADE OF MATERIAL OTHER THAN ALUMINUM, WILL SERVE AS A GOOD STEAMER BASKET.

LID

VEGGIES

TOP OF TWO PART PAN

BOTTOM OF PAN

WATER

"SPAGHETTI COOKERS" MAKE GREAT VEGETABLE STEAMERS ENAMEL, DARK BLUE WITH WHITE FLECKS, BIG AND CHEAP.

SOME TIPS ON COOKING

Baking: Try to combine things that take an e-
qual amount of time to bake. This gives you a
wide choice since roots, onions, tubers and
squash take equal time. Large pieces mixed
with a bit of oil can take from 30-45 min. at
375°, medium pieces take 30 min. at 375° and
small pieces only 20-25 min. at 375°. I don't
usually bake any of the cabbage family except
in a few casseroles. They're much better
steamed or sauteed, if cooked at all, leafy
greens are the same. Mushrooms can go anywhere
it seems. Although the taste is altered by
the way they're cooked, the flavor is always
satisfactory. Add tamari, salt or gomasio.

Sauteeing: Most vegetables saute at different
speeds but this can be grouped easily. I always start my onions and garlic first in a little oil (1 T. for small bunch, 2 T. for more).
Stir and saute for a minute or 2 depending on
the size of pieces. Next add carrot or any
other root including burdock which doesn't need
to cook any longer than carrot. The only exception I can think of is lotus root which takes
longer than onions and should be added 5 min.
before. After the roots have cooked covered
2-3 min., add squash and cook covered 2-3 more
min. Next comes the cabbage family. Stir and
cover 5-7 min. Add mushrooms and greens, cover
and finish in 2-3 min. more. If it sounds com-
plicated, once you do it a few times, it gets
easy. Add a little tamari, salt or gomasio at
the end of cooking.

Steaming: Any vegetable that can be cooked can
be steamed. It works best to slice thin and
not too big pieces. I rarely steam anything
more than 10-15 min. and that is mostly onions,
roots, plants in the cabbage family and squash.
Leafy greens, mushrooms and light vegetables I
cook 5-7 min. Sometimes I only just wilt greens
for a min. under a cover.

MISO VEGETABLES

Follow directions for sauteed vegetables, add
1-2 T. miso and mix in at the end of cooking.

CARROTS AND ONIONS WITH TEKKA

1 lb. carrots, sliced
1 lg. onion
2 T. tekka
2 T. oil
1 T. tamari

Heat oil and add onion, saute a min. and add
carrot and tekka. Stir it up and cook covered
over med. heat for 10 min. or until carrots are
just tender. Add tamari if you like and stir.
(enough for 6 side dish portions)

Other vegetables can be sauted with tekka. Substitute or add more to the carrot-onion recipe.

SESAME VEGETABLES

Use basic recipe on sauteed vegetables (on opp-
osite page) but before adding oil to pan roast
2-4 T. sesame seeds until brown and crumbly.
Sunflower seeds can be used the same way.

CURRIED VEGETABLES

Heat 2 T. curry powder in 2 T. oil for a min.
Add 1 lg. chopped onion, 2 sliced carrots, 1/2
head broccoli, cut green beans (1/4 lb.) and
sliced radishes (2-3 lg.). Saute until just
tender and add tamari.
Lemon juice (from 1 lemon) is good added to it.
Try adding a pint of yoghurt and heat just to
eating temperature. (6 side portions)

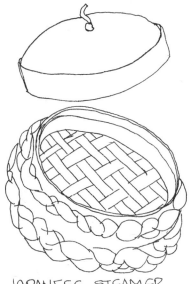

JAPANESE STEAMER

VEGETABLES ARE LAID ON
THE INNER WOVEN STRIPS, AND
THE STEAMER IS SET OVER
BOILING WATER IN BOTTOM
OF WOK. THESE STEAMERS
CAN BE STACKED TO STEAM
MANY FOODS SEPARATELY,
BUT AT THE SAME TIME.

BURDOCK AND CABBAGE

3 big or 6 small burdock roots well scrubbed
  and sliced thin
1 lg. head green cabbage shredded or cut thin
2 T. oil
2 T. tamari

Heat 2 T. oil and saute burdock 5 min., stirring
first then covering. Add cabbage and cook covered 5-7 min. Add tamari and eat. (6)

SAUTEED EGGPLANT AND ZUCCHINI

1 lg. onion or 1 big bunch scallions
2 sm. or 1 lg. eggplant
3 sm. zucchini
2 cloves garlic, crushed
2 T. oil
2 T. tamari
1 t. basil

Heat oil and add garlic and onion for 2-3 min.
Put in the zucchini and eggplant and cover for
10 min. Add basil for the last 2-3 min. of
cooking. Serve with tamari to taste. (6 portions)
Add tomatoes for last 5 min. if you want.
Melt cheese on it during last 5 min.

SAUTEED JERUSALEM ARTICHOKES

1 lg. onion
2-3 stalks parsley
1 lb. artichokes
2 T. oil
tamari

Heat oil and stir in onion a min. Add artichokes and stir. Cover and cook over med. heat
for 10-15 min. until vegetables are tender.
Add 1 t. salt and eat. (4 servings)

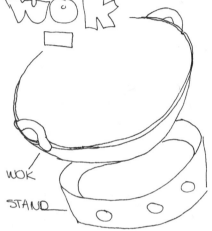

WOK

WOK
STAND

THE
CHINESE ALL-PURPOSE PAN
FOR STEAMING, SAUTEEING,
FRYING, TEMPURA...
SHOULD BE MADE OF HEAVY
STEEL FOR BEST COOKING.
USED IN A STAND OR
DIRECTLY ON FLAME.

GLOBE ARTICHOKES WITH LEMON SOY-BUTTER

Steam 2 med. sized artichokes in a little water
for 20 min. Serve whole and pull off leaves to
eat after dipping them in a sauce of 1 t. ground
mustard roasted till brown. Add lemon juice of
3 lemons and 2 c. salted soy butter. Mix well
and serve.
It's a nice vegetable to eat along with dinner
or just eat by itself. And don't forget to
eat the heart, it's the best part. Discard the
feathery cluster that sits on the heart and
eat the tender center. The heart is good in
salad, too.

GLOBE ARTICHOKE
A MEMBER OF THE
THISTLE FAMILY.

JERUSALEM ARTICHOKE PANCAKES

Don't expect these to be like potato pancakes.
Jerusalem artichokes are much sweeter because
they are not a starchy vegetable. Follow the
potato pancake recipe using 1 1/2 lb. Jerusalem
artichokes instead of potatoes. They're not
the same, but just as good.

MIXED VEGETABLES IN GINGER-ARROWROOT SAUCE

1 med. onion
1 carrot
2 sm. kohlrabi with leaves (if possible)
2 stalks celery
1 zucchini
2 stalks broccoli
2-3 stalks of some green (mustard, beet or some-
    thing)
2 cloves garlic, crushed
2 T. grated fresh ginger
4 round T. arrowroot flour or starch
2 c. water
2 T. tamari
1 T. oil

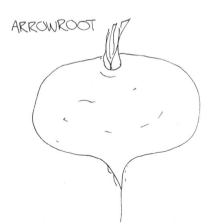

ARROWROOT

LARGE, ROUND, LIGHT BROWN
ROOT. CAN BE USED FRESH
AS A VEGETABLE AND
IS SIMILAR TO A POTATO
IN CONSISTENCY BUT
MUCH SWEETER . ARROW-
ROOT FLOUR IS USED AS A
THICKENER FOR CLEAR SAUCES

Heat oil and add garlic, onion and ginger and
stir a min. Toss in carrot and kohlrabi for
2-3 min. Then mix in broccoli, zucchini and
celery. Cook 5 min. covered. Add greens,
water and arrowroot dissolved in 1/4 c. cold
water. Heat and stir until thick and add tamari. Serve on rice or noodles. (for 6)

EGG CORN FRITTERS

3 eggs, separate
2 c. corn or corn from 6 ears
2 c. whole wheat pastry or other fine flour
1 1/2 c. water
1 t. salt

Mix everything but egg white together. Beat
whites stiff and turn into batter. Drop in
360° oil for 3-5 min. until golden.
If you have time to chill batter a few hours,
the fritters cook even better.
Add 1/2 c. sesame seeds to batter.
Add a chopped onion.
For a sweet trip, add 1/2 c. honey.

NO-EGG CORN FRITTERS

2 c. cornmeal
2 c. corn or corn from 6 ears
1 c. whole wheat pastry or other light flour
1/2 c. soy butter if possible or 1/4 c. oil
1 t. salt
1 1/2 c. water

Mix till smooth and drop into oil (360°) until
golden. Any variation of egg fritters can be
used as well as any vegetable. In addition,
it's good to let this batter sit out 12-24
hours. Chill it for 2 hours until good and
cold then cook it in oil. Cooking can also be
done without oil on a well seasoned iron skillet. Just bake patties over med. flame until
well browned on both sides. You can even add
cheese to the top of each pattie, cooking covered while second side browns.

SWEET AND SOUR VEGETABLES

Saute vegetables like mixed vegetables in gin-
ger-arrowroot sauce recipe but substitute apple
juice for water or water plus 1/2 c. apple concentrate. Add 1/4 lb. currants or raisins with
carrots. At the end add lemon from 2 lemons
with tamari. (enough for 6 servings on rice)

GINGER

BAKED MAPLE-CARROTS

Make carrot sticks of 1 lb. carrots. Mix in
baking dish with 1/2 c. maple syrup and 2 T.
oil. Bake 25 min. at 350°. If you can't cover
it, stir it a few times while it bakes. Un-
cover for the last 10 min. of baking.

CABBAGE WITH CARAWAY CREAM SAUCE

1 med. head cabbage
2 c. med. white sauce
1 t. caraway seeds
1 T. tamari

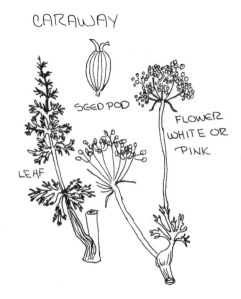

CARAWAY

SEED POD

FLOWER
WHITE OR
PINK

LEAF

Steam cabbage cut in quarters for 10 min. Mix
the caraway seeds and tamari with the warm
white sauce. Put a piece of cabbage on plate
and pour sauce over it. (for 4)
If you make this for a big group, place quartered cabbage in a deep baking pan, cover with
a proportionate amount of sauce and bake covered in a 375° oven for 20 min.
Put mushrooms in, it's good.
It's also good without the caraway seeds.

DILLED CARROTS

1 lb. carrots
2 T. dill weed
1 T. oil
1/2 c. water

Heat oil and add sliced carrots. Stir a min.,
add water and cook covered over med. flame for
10 min. Add dill and steam a couple min. more
until carrots are just tender.
You can add salt if you want but it's really
not necessary.

SWEET PEPPER

AVOCADO-CHILI FILLING

2 small soft avocados
1 sweet red pepper
1 hot green or red pepper or 1/2 t. cayenne
1 clove garlic
2 T. lemon and oil mixture
2 t. paprika
1 t. salt
chopped mushroom stems

Mash avocado until smooth. Add the other ingredients and fill mushrooms.
Serve plain or on a bed of sprouts.

COTTAGE CHEESE AND TOMATO FILLING

Fill caps with cottage cheese and pour tomato
sauce made from:
6 chopped tomatoes
1 small green pepper
1 lg. onion
chopped mushroom stems
2 cloves garlic, crushed
2 T. olive oil
1 t. oregano
1/2 t. basil

Saute onion and garlic in olive oil. After a
min. add pepper, tomato and herbs. Simmer covered for 20 min. Pour over stuffed mushrooms
and bake 10 min. at 400°.

CELERY

CELERY-NUT STUFFING

1 small bunch celery with tops
chopped mushroom tops
1 bunch scallions
1/2 lb. chopped nuts (almonds, cashews)
2 T. lemon-oil mixture
2 T. tamari

Fill mushrooms and pour extra lemon and oil
over top. Bake the same as the others.

BAKED CREAMED ONION WITH NUTMEG

3 lg. onions sliced
2 c. white sauce (thin)
1 t. nutmeg, grated
2 T. oil
1/2 t. salt

Saute onion 1 min. in oil. Add sauce, nutmeg
and salt. Mix and bake 15 min. at 400°.
(enough for 4)

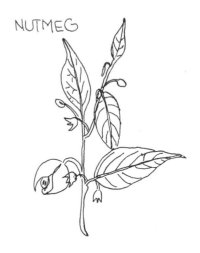

NUTMEG

SCALLOPED POTATOES WITH MILK

4-5 big potatoes, sliced thin
1 lg. onion, sliced
4 c. fresh milk
1 t. salt
paprika

Layer onions and potatoes in oiled baking dish.
Sprinkle with salt, pour milk over top and
sprinkle with paprika. Bake 30 min. at 375°.

NO-MILK SCALLOPED POTATOES

Follow milk recipe substituting 1 c. tahini
and 4 c. water for milk. Bake the same.
Other vegetables may be added - parsley, mushrooms, peas.

BAKED CHEESE AND POTATOES

Slice potatoes the same as for scalloped potatoes. Saute with or without onion in 2 T. oil
until almost tender. Put in baking dish, with
layers of cheddar or some cheese in between.
Pour 2 c. milk, tahini and water, or stock over
mixture and bake for 25 min. at 375°. (for 6)

PEAS AND POTATOES

Boil 2 lbs. potatoes with skins until tender.
Mash with 1/2 c. thick milk or cream, 2 T. oil
or butter, 1 t. salt, 2 t. chervil (if possible). Add 2 c. fresh peas, mix and bake in
oiled dish 15 min. at 400°. (enough for 6)

TURNING OR FOLDING IN

IS A TERM FOR A SPECIAL WAY OF STIRRING ONE FOOD INTO ANOTHER BY LIFTING THE FIRST FOOD FROM THE BOTTOM OF THE BOWL AND FOLDING IT OVER THE SECOND FOOD. THIS MOTION IS REPEATED UNTIL BOTH FOODS ARE MIXED.

RADISH

POTATO PANCAKES   (Also known as Latkes)

3 lg. potatoes
1 lg. onion
6 eggs, separate
2 T. tamari
1 t. caraway seeds

Scrub potato and grate skins and all. Either grate or chop the onion. Crush caraway and add along with yolks and tamari. Mix well and turn in stiffly beaten white of egg. Cook till golden brown on each side in an oiled heavy skillet. Eat with butter, honey, maple syrup, sour cream, or yoghurt.

STEWED WATERMELON RIND

Peel off outer skin from rind of watermelon. It's okay if there's a little pink left on rind Put in a heavy pan, add a sprinkle of salt and water to cover the bottom of the pan. Cover and simmer 20 min. until rind is tender. Drain and add butter, salt or tamari.
Grate rind and chop one lg. onion. Saute with dill, sage, basil or favorite herb until tender. Eat it like a vegetable.

GERMAN POTATOES

Cut into pieces 2 lb. of potatoes with skins. Boil until soft. Slice and arrange in oiled baking pan. Heat 2 T. oil and add to it 1 lg. sliced onion and cook 5 min. Stir in 1/2 lb. chopped mushrooms, 1/2 t. hot red pepper flakes, 1/4 c. apple cider vinegar, 2 T. tamari, 1/4 c. oil and 1/2 c. water. Stir together and cover potatoes with it. Bake at 375° for 20 min. Roast sesame seeds before adding oil to pan for sauteeing the onion.

CREAMED RADISHES

Steam 2 lbs. of little red radishes in water for 10 min. Put in an oiled baking dish, cover with 3 c. med. white sauce and bake at 375° for 15 min. Radishes get tender and mild when cooked.

STEWED CUCUMBER

6 cucumbers
2 T. oil
2 T. tamari
1 c. thin white sauce
flour

Cut cucumbers in thick slices and saute in oil
until golden. Pour white sauce over them and
2 T. tamari. Simmer together 10 min. (enough
for 6)

CREAMED CUCUMBER AND GINGER

Cut 4 cucumbers in pieces. Saute with 2 t.
fresh grated ginger and 1 lg. chopped onion for
2-3 min. Pour 2 c. med. white sauce made with
thick milk or cream and simmer 5 min. Sprinkle
with paprika.

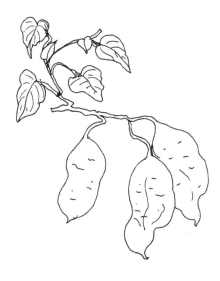

SWEET POTATO

SWEET POTATO CUTLETS

Add 1/2 c. chopped pecans or other nut to 4 c.
mashed sweet potatoes. Shape into patties,
roll in chopped nuts, place in oiled baking
pan and sprinkle the tops with a little oil.
Bake at 450° for 20 min. (makes 8 lg. patties)
Serve plain, with honey or maple syrup, butter,
vegetable sauce, tomato sauce or mushroom gravy.

SWEET POTATO CROQUETTES

4 med. size sweet potatoes
2 T. oil or soy butter
2 T. honey
1/4 t. cayenne
1 t. salt

Bake the sweet potatoes at 400° for 35 min.
Mash, add oil, salt, cayenne, and honey and
beat. Shape into little eggs and roll in mixture of 1/2 cornmeal and 1/2 flour. Fry in
deep oil at 375° for 3-4 min. Drain.
(8-10 croquettes)
Add chopped nuts before frying, or onion or
sprouts.

STUFFED CELERY

Get large stalks of celery and serve with leaves
and all. Fill the large hollow part with cream
cheese and bryndza (a crumbly sheep's milk
cheese).

1 8 oz. package goat cream cheese
1 8 oz. c. bryndza or any other sharp grating
   cheese (romano, parmesano)
1 med. onion, chopped fine
juice of 1 lemon
1/4 c. water

Let cream cheese get soft and add other ingredients to it. Salt to taste.

STEAMED GREENS

Chop greens and steam in boiling water for 7-
10 min. Or stick over boiling water until
greens just wilt, then eat.

MISO-ONION SPREAD

walnut size piece of miso
3/4 c. tahini
1 lg. onion, sauted 5 min. in 1 T. oil
juice of 2 lemons
1 T. tamari
1/4 c. warm water (for softening miso)

Mix everything together and stuff celery.
You can stuff celery with anything you want.

EGGLESS TEMPURA BATTER

1 c. whole wheat pastry or rice flour
2 c. corn flour, cornmeal or half and half
1/4 c. arrowroot
1 t. salt
3 3/4 c. cold water

Mix together and chill well or work with an ice
cube in the batter. Dip vegetables in batter
and fry in 350-365° oil until golden brown.
Drain well and eat.

SPINACH

MUSTARD

YELLOW FLOWER
CLUSTERS
PRECEDE THE
SEEDS USED FOR
SPICING. THE
ENTIRE PLANT IS
EDIBLE FROM EARLY
SHOOTS UNTIL THE
FLOWERS BLOOM.

EGG TEMPURA

2 1/2 c. whole wheat pastry or rice flour
3 eggs, separate
2 2/3 c. water
1 t. salt

Beat egg whites until stiff. Mix all other ingredients together and turn in egg whites. Use
the same as in eggless recipe.
In both tempuras, it is best to work with cold
batter and vegetables for crisp, light tempura.
The oil should be between 350-365° and never
smoke. Oil can be reused. If oil gets cloudy,
clear it by dropping an umeboshi plum in it.

CHEESE TEMPURA

Cut any cheese in little cubes or bricks. Dip
in tempura batter and cook only a min. all together.

MIXED VEGETABLE TEMPURA   (Vegetenanda)

Mix chopped up vegetables with tempura batter.
Chill well and drop by spoonful into hot oil
Makes little vegetable patties.

Raw: carrots
       celery
       mushrooms
       beets
       lettuce
       cucumber
       radish
       cabbage
       cauliflower
       broccoli
       summer squash
       any leafy greens

Almost any vegetable can be eaten raw with the
exception of a few starchy root vegetables and
hard above ground kinds. Slice in shapes that
please you.

KOHLRABI
TUBER THAT GROWS ABOVE
GROUND. LIGHT, SWEET
VEGETABLE--GOOD FOR
STEAMING OR SAUTEEING.

5
GRAINS

OATMEAL
(ROLLED OATS)

TINY FLAT FLAKES USED AS A BREAKFAST CEREAL, COOKED OR RAW AND USED IN BAKING.

STEEL-CUT OATS

COARSELY CHOPPED WHOLE OATS

RICE CREAM

FINELY GROUND RICE, ROASTED TO A NUTTY FLAVOR.

CRACKED WHEAT

WHOLE GRAIN WHEAT, COARSELY CRACKED, RATHER THAN GROUND LIKE FLOUR.

OATMEAL

Bring 2 1/2 c. of water, soy or nut milk to a boil. Add a pinch of salt and a c. of rolled oats. Cook covered for 10 min. and let sit for 10.
Along with oats you can add raisins, sunflower seeds or other dry nuts or fruits. Cinnamon, nutmeg...cook it and add honey while it sits. (enough for 2 big people, 4 little ones)

STEEL-CUT OATS

Roast 1 c. steel-cut oats in dry pan until they're brown. Add 2 1/2 c. water and boil covered 30 min. They may be used in recipes for rolled oats. Sesame seeds can be roasted with the oats and cooked. (serves 4)

RICE CREAM

Roast the rice cream until light brown. Bring 1 c. of it and 4 c. of water to a boil over flame in the top half of a double boiler. Put over boiling water in bottom half and cook for 30 min. Turn off and let sit over water for 30 min.
If you add dry fruits or nuts do it during the sitting time.

CRACKED WHEAT

Take 1 c. fresh cracked wheat and add to 3 c. boiling water and a bit of salt. Cook covered for 20 min. Turn off and let sit for 10. Any fruits or nuts can be cooked with it.

CEREAL FLAKES (Rice, Wheat, and Rye)

Add 1 c. of the flakes to 2 1/2 c. boiling water, 1 T. oil and a pinch of salt. Cook covered for 15 min. and let sit 15 min. before uncovering. Flakes can be used like oatmeal. (enough for 2 big folks and 4 little)

FLAKED CORN

You need 3 c. boiling water, 2 T. oil, and a pinch or 2 of salt. Add 1 c. of flaked corn and boil slowly covered for 30 min. Turn off fire and let it sit for 15 min. before eating. This is good for any meal.

GRANOLA

Mix together in a big bowl:
1 lb. rolled oats
1/2 c. millet
1/2 c. sesame seeds
1 lb. wheat or rye flakes
1/2 c. sunflower seeds
1/2 c. buckwheat or kasha or both
1/2 lb. chopped cashews or almonds
1 c. honey mixed with 3/4 c. oil
2 c. coconut

Mix until everything is evenly coated with honey and oil. Bake at 250°, stirring now and again, for 2-3 hours depending on how brown you want it. Remove from oven and add 1 lb. currants or raisins or both.
If you prefer not to roast it, add the fruit after mixing and store. It's nice to keep refrigerated if it's not to be eaten within a week.

BROWN RICE

1 c. rice
2 1/2 c. water
1 T. oil
1/2 t. salt

Wash rice well. Bring to boil with water, oil and salt. Simmer, covered for 40 min., until water is absorbed. Turn off flame and allow to sit 10 min. before uncovering. (makes about 3 c. cooked rice)
Before adding water to rice, roast it with or without oil until golden brown and cook as above. Roast 2-3 T. sesame seeds with the rice, too, if you like and cook as above.

FLAKED GRAINS

GRAINS WHICH ARE ROLLED IN HUGE PRESSES AND SQUASHED FLAT LIKE ROLLED OATS.

OATS

GRANOLA

CAN BE A MIXTURE OF ANY GRAINS, DRY FRUIT, NUTS, SEEDS... I ROAST MINE, BUT IT'S NOT NECESSARY. INCREASE THE HONEY FOR UNROASTED GRANOLA.

BROWN RICE

WHOLE GRAIN
UNPROCESSED FOOD.
ORIGINALLY COMES
FROM THE ORIENT,
BUT IT IS NOW
GROWN IN SEVERAL
SOUTHERN STATES
AND CALIFORNIA

RICE

MUNG BEANS AND RICE

1 c. mung beans
1 c. rice
10 c. water
1 t. salt
1/4 c. olive oil (butter or ghee may be used)
4 cloves garlic, crushed
1 T. turmeric
1 t. cayenne
1 T. cumin seed
2 T. paprika
1 t. oregano
1/2 t. basil
1 t. savory
tamari

Mung beans should be washed and soaked several hours or overnight in the water. Bring to boil and cook 1 hour. Heat garlic, turmeric, cayenne, cumin and paprika in olive oil and add to beans along with rice and salt. Cook slowly for 2 hours and add herbs and tamari. (makes enough for 8)
Sauteed vegetables may be added for the last 15 min. of cooking. Yoghurt is also a good addition.

LENTIL RICE

2 c. rice
1 c. lentils
2 cloves garlic
2 carrots
1 onion
1 t. tarragon
1 t. fennel seeds
9 c. water
2 T. oil
1 t. salt
tamari

Combine rice, lentils, water and fennel seeds heated slightly in 1 T. of the oil. Boil gently for 1 hour. Saute garlic, onion and carrot in 1 T. of oil and add to rice along with salt. Simmer 15 min., stir in tarragon and tamari to taste and allow to steam, off the flame, 10 min. Mix well and serve.

SESAME FRIED RICE

2 c. cooked rice
2 T. sesame seeds
2 T. vegetable oil
1 T. tamari

Roast sesame seeds dry until nutty brown. Add
oil and rice and stir fry until rice and sesame
seeds are mixed together. Add tamari and eat.

LEMON-HIZIKI RICE

2 c. cooked rice
juice of 2 lemons
1 c. cooked hiziki (seaweed)
2 T. oil
tamari to taste

Add all ingredients except lemon to heated oil.
Stir fry until hot and well mixed. Stir in
lemon juice. (serves 4)

FRIED RICE AND CHICKPEAS

2 c. cooked rice
1 c. cooked chickpeas
1 lg. onion
2 T. tamari
2 T. tahini
1/2 t. dill seed
1/4 c. water
2 t. caraway seed
1 T. paprika
2 T. oil

Lightly saute onions with caraway, paprika and
dill until onions are golden and clear. Add
rice and chickpeas and stir fry until well
mixed. Blend together tamari, tahini, and water. Pour over rice and mix together.
(serves 4)
A squeeze or two of lemon is a fine addition
to this.

THERE IS SHORT, MEDIUM OR LONG GRAIN BROWN RICE. IT IS A MATTER OF FLAVOR AND CONSISTENCY IN CHOOSING.

LONG GRAIN
LONG, THIN COOKS SOFTER AND TASTES MILDER THAN SHORT-GRAIN.

MEDIUM
SLIGHTLY LONGER THAN SHORT

SHORT
FAT, ROUND LITTLE GRAIN. COOKS UP FIRM AND HAS A GOOD STRONG FLAVOR.

TAHINI-TAMARI FRIED RICE

2 c. cooked rice
2 T. tamari
2 T tahini
1 T. oil

Add rice, tamari and tahini to oil and stir fry until well mixed and hot. (serves 2)

ADUKI RICE

2 c. rice
1 c. aduki beans
9 c. water
2 T. oil
1 t. salt

Cook aduki beans, water and oil for 1 1/2 hours. Add rice and salt and continue to cook 40 min. more. Allow it to sit covered 10 min.
(makes 8-10 cups)

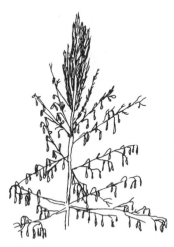

WILD RICE

BAKED CREAMED PEAS AND RICE

Cook 2 c. of roasted rice in 5 c. of water as in the basic recipe. While it cooks, saute 1 lg. onion in 1 T. oil for 1-2 min. Add 2 c. of fresh regular peas or snow peas and saute 5 min. longer. Remove from the pan to a bowl. To the pan add 6 T. whole wheat pastry flour or other fine ground flour, and 6 T. oil. Stir to a paste and add slowly 1 c. boiling water or stock. Stir smooth, then add 1 more c. boiling liquid. When thickened and smooth mix peas and cooked rice with it. Put into greased baking dish and bake it at 400° for 20 min. Sprinkle with gomasio (sesame salt) just before it's done. Eat hot, or chill it and eat it cold with your favorite kind of salad dressing. Bleu cheese dressing is great. (serves 6)

MONTEZUMA RICE BALLS

2 c. cooked rice
2 T. tamari
oil for deep frying

This works best when rice is cooked with 3 c.
water until slightly mushy for 45-60 min. Mix
with tamari and, dipping hands in cold water to
prevent sticking, press rice into little balls,
no bigger than a walnut. Heat oil to 350° and
drop 3 or 4 balls in at a time, frying until
golden. They should fry in about 1 min. on
each side or else the oil is not hot enough.
Drain in basket or on brown paper.
(8-10 little balls)

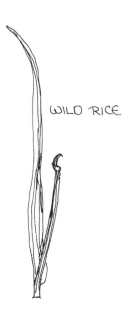

WILD RICE

Add to basic mixture:
1) umeboshi plum slivers for a slightly sour
   taste (these plum slivers will act as a pre-
   servative in any of the rice ball combinations, so you can take them traveling for a
   munchy).
   You'll use 1-2 plums for each 2 c. cooked
   rice in recipe.
2) 1/2 c. cooked aduki beans
3) 1/4 c. sesame seeds
4) 2 T. tahini
5) 1/2 c. onions and carrots or other vegetable
   combinations
6) 1/2 c. dry currants
7) 1/2 c. chopped nuts
8) parsley
9) 1 t. savory, dill, chervil, sage or other
   herbs, or a mixture of 2 or 3
10) 1/2 c. cooked, mashed chick peas
11) or combine 2-3 ingredients from the above
    list

MISO RICE

Cook rice as you would in basic recipe. For
every c. of uncooked rice use 2 round T. miso.
When rice has cooked and all water is dissolved,
stir in miso softened in water. Cover again
and immediately remove from heat. Allow to sit
10 min. before serving.

GARLIC FRIED RICE

2 c. cooked rice
2 cloves garlic, mashed and chopped
2 T. oil
tamari

Saute garlic in oil for 5 min. Add rice and tamari and stir until mixed and hot.

RICE AND PARSLEY SQUARES WITH MUSHROOM CREAM SAUCE

Take 4 c. of cooked brown rice, mix it with 1/4 c. oil and 1 c. fresh parsley or 1/2 c. dry parsley. Mix well and bake in square or round greased pan at 400° for 20 min. Allow to set for a bit before slicing. While it cooks, heat 2 T. oil in a pan and add 1 bunch scallions, leeks, or 1 lg. onion. Saute 2-3 min. and add 1/2 lb. mushrooms and saute 2 more min., put it in a bowl. Add 6 T. rice flour, buckwheat or wholewheat flour and 6 T. oil to pan and stir smooth. Add 1 c. boiling stock or other liquid to paste and stir until smooth. Add second c. of liquid to sauce and stir until thick and smooth. Add 2 T. tamari. Cut rice into 4 squares and serve on plates with sauce and mushrooms poured over the top. (4 portions)

COCONUT PALM

CURRIED-COCONUT RICE

Have 6 c. cooked brown rice, preferably cold. Heat 2 T. curry powder in 2 T. oil for a min. Add 1 lg. onion, 2 carrots, 1 c. unsweetened coconut or 1 1/2 c. fresh grated coconut. Mix, cover and cook on med. flame for 10 min. Add the rice, mix well with 3 T. tamari and 1 c. mung or alfalfa sprouts. Eat with 3 others.

KASHA AND BUCKWHEAT

The way I like to cook buckwheat groats and
kasha is to mix half of each, but you may prefer to eat them individually as they both have
distinct and different flavors. When cooking
the raw buckwheat, it's tastier to roast it until brown in oil before adding water. The basic recipe I use is a never-mushy one. Buckwheat or kasha get soft and sticky very easily,
maybe you will prefer it that way, but I like
the grains to be separate and light.

1/2 c. raw buckwheat
1/2 c. kasha (roasted buckwheat, dark)
2 c. water
2 T. oil
1 t. salt

BUCKWHEAT

Bring water to boil, add grains, oil and salt.
Return to slow boil and cook 10 min. Do not
lift cover, and remove from flame. Allow to
sit 10 min. before serving. It can be eaten
with vegetables, with butter and tamari, or
even as a cereal with milk and/or butter and
honey. (makes 3 c. of cooked grain)

SUNFLOWER FRIED KASHA

Prepare as above omitting tahini and roasting
1/4 c. sunflower seeds in oil before adding
onion.

TAHINI-ONION FRIED KASHA

2 c. cooked kasha
1 med. onion
2 T. tahini
2 T. tamari
2 T. oil

Saute onion in oil slightly. Add kasha, tahini
and tamari. Stir fry until well mixed.

FLINT CORN

ONE OF THE HARD CORNS GROUND FOR CORN MEAL.

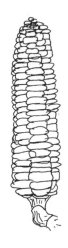

DENT CORN

A HARD CORN FOR GRINDING.

BODHISATTVA BUCKWHEAT BURGERS

2 c. cooked kasha
1 med. onion, chopped
1/2 c. whole wheat flour
2 T. tamari
oil
little water if necessary

Mix ingredients except oil and press into patties. Wet hands with cold water to keep from sticking. Put a little oil in pan and cook on med. flame until brown on both sides and done in the middle.

KASHA CORNMEAL CAKES

2 c. cooked kasha
1/2 c. buckwheat flour
2 c. cornmeal
2 T. tamari
2 T. tahini
2 T. oil

Mix together with enough water to make a sticky batter. Spread in round patties on lightly greased skillet. Brown on one side and turn, browning second side until cooked through.

KASHA-MUSHROOM BURGERS

Saute 1/2 lb. sliced mushrooms, 2 cloves chopped garlic, and 1 lg. onion in 2 T. oil for 5 min. Add this, 1/4 c. tahini, and 3 T. tamari to 4 c. cooked kasha. Shape into patties and fry in oil until brown on both sides. (makes about 8 burgers)
It's best to have mushy kasha for this recipe. Use 3 c. water in cooking kasha.

BAKED KASHA AND VEGETABLES

4 c. cooked kasha
2 stalks celery
1/2 head cabbage (red, green or 1/4 of each)
2 med. beets
1 lg. onion
tamari
oil

Dice beets and saute in 1 T. oil until almost
cooked but not mushy. Remove and set aside.
Wipe wok (or skillet). Heat 1 T. oil with caraway seeds and first add onion then celery
and cabbage. First stir, then cover for 3-4
min. Mix the kasha and vegetables (except
beets) along with tamari to taste. Add beets
last stirring only sufficiently to mix together.
Bake in lightly oiled casserole for 25 min. at
350°.
For a creamy casserole, add 1 pt. yoghurt, 1 t.
salt and 3 stalks chopped parsley to kasha-ve-
getable mixture and bake as above.

KASHA MEATLESS LOAF

2 c. cooked kasha
1 c. buckwheat flour or corn flour
1 lg. onion
4 sprigs parsley
1/2 c. cooked aduki beans
1 clove garlic
1/4 t. basil
2 T. tahini
tamari
water if needed

PARSLEY

Chop onion, parsley and garlic into fine pieces. Mix with kasha, aduki beans, tahini,
flour, tamari and water to make thick sticky
dough. Place in greased bread pan and bake at
325° for 1-1 1/2 hours until deep golden brown
and solid to the touch. Slice and serve it
plain or with miso gravy.

AUTUMN HASH

4 c. cooked kasha
1/2 of a butternut squash
1 lg. onion
1 lg. sweet potato
1 carrot
2 T. oil
3 T. tamari

Saute chopped vegetables in oil, starting with onion then adding carrot for 2-3 min., then squash and sweet potato. Cook covered over med. heat until vegetables are cooked through but not too soft. Stir fry in the kasha and tamari until hot. (serves 6-8)

SCALLOPED KASHA AND POTATOES

Saute 4 lg. sliced potatoes, 2 lg. sliced onions in 3 T. oil for 5 min. Add 1 c. raw kasha and 2 T. paprika and stir together. Pour 5 c. water mixed with 1 c. of tahini and bake at 400° for 25 min. in greased square or circle. (4 large servings)

KASHA AND POTATOES

Prepare 6 c. cooked kasha. Heat 3 T. oil (olive is great). Add 1 lg. onion and 6 sliced potatoes to it and saute 5 min. Cover and cook until potatoes are done. Add the kasha, 3 T. tamari and stir together. (eat with 3 others)

KASHA PIE AND MASHED POTATOES

Take the mushroom burger mixture and put it in a pie pan. Decorate the top with 6 med. potatoes, skins and all, mashed with 1/4 c. cream and 1/2 t. sea salt and maybe 2 T. parsley or 1 T. dill weed, or 2 T. crushed caraway seeds. Bake at 375° for 20 min. Slice it into 6 sections.

KASHA KNISHES

If you have leftovers make kasha knishes. Mix leftover kasha with a couple chopped onions and cloves of garlic (smashed and chopped), a bit of oil to moisten, and tamari to taste. Roasted sesame seeds are good, too. Make a pie dough like the basic recipe. (If you have one that works for you, use it). Roll out pretty thin like a pie and put kasha in center. Lift sides of dough over the top, kind of cupping your hands, and shape it into a nice round little ball. Put on a greased sheet and bake about 25 min. at 350-375°. Just before they're done, brush the tops well with oil and let them brown nicely the last 10 min. Eat 'em hot or take them on a trip. You might want to mix some umeboshi plum pieces in the kasha to help preserve them if you'll be out several days. Use kasha and potatoes to fill knishes.

MILLET

1 c. uncooked millet
1/2 t. salt
2 c. water
1 T. oil

Dry roast millet in heavy pan until golden brown and nutty smelling. Add 2 c. boiling water, salt, and oil. Cover and cook over low flame for 25 min. Turn off and allow to sit 10 min.
If you don't feel like roasting the millet, it's good without, too.

KNISHES

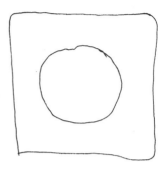

ROLL DOUGH TO RECTANGLE AND CUT INTO SQUARES (ABOUT 4"). IN CENTER OF EACH SQUARE, PLACE KASHA. FOLD EACH CORNER TO CENTER AND SEAL THE ENDS TOGETHER. WITH CUPPED HANDS SHAPE INTO ROUND PASTRY.

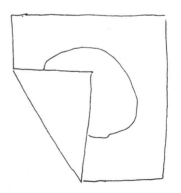

Grains 91

ROASTED MILLET AND VEGETABLE PIE

1 c. millet roasted with 2 T. sesame seeds
pie crust for top and bottom
1 lg. onion
1 green pepper
1 zucchini or yellow summer squash
1 stalk broccoli
2 cloves garlic
3 T. oil
2 T. tamari
2 1/2 c. water

Cook millet, 1 T. oil and water according to
basic directions. Heat 2 T. oil and saute vegetables starting with garlic and onion, then
add remaining veggies. Toss over med.-high
heat for a min. or two. Mix in cooked millet
and tamari and fill large pie shell. Cover
with top crust, brush with oil. Bake 25 min.
at 375°. (serves 6)
Add 2 T. tahini to millet and vegetables for
a creamy pie.

MILLET BURGERS

2 c. cooked millet
3 T. tahini
1 c. buckwheat flour
2 cloves garlic, mashed and chopped
1 lg. onion
3 T. tamari

Chop onion, mix all ingredients and add water
if it's needed to make a sticky batter. Spread
patties onto lightly greased skillet and cook
over med.-high flame until golden brown on both
sides and done through. Don't make them real
thick or they stay raw in the middle.

BAKED MILLET AND ONIONS

Saute 3 lg. onions in 2 T. oil for 5 min. Add
1 green pepper and cook a min. Mix with 5 c.
roasted cooked millet and 2 T. tamari. Put in
an oiled bake pan and bake 20 min. at 400°.
(6 slices)

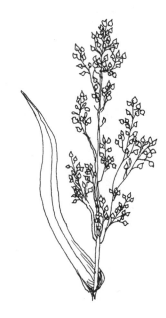

MILLET

SYRIAN LENTILS AND MILLET

Add 1 c. of millet and 1 c. syrian lentils to
6 c. boiling water and 2 T. oil (olive oil is
nice). Let the mixture boil slowly 20 min.
Add to it 1 lg. onion, 1 green pepper, 1 t. cumin, 1/8 t. cayenne, 2 bay leaves and 1/2 t.
oregano sauteed 5 min. in 2 T. oil. Simmer
together 15 min. Add tamari to taste.
(serves 6-8)

BARLEY

1 c. barley
3 c. water
1 t. salt

Roast barley until light golden. Add boiling
water, cover and let cook over low heat for 30
min. or until water is absorbed. Turn off and
let sit for 10 min. You don't have to roast
this one, just cook it plain, but it has a
nutty flavor if you do roast it.

BARLEY AND LENTILS

Bring 1 c. barley and 1 c. green lentils to a
boil in 6 c. of water and 2 T. oil. Cook for
1 1/2 hours or until water is absorbed. Good
with tamari.
Herbs like dill, caraway and cumin seeds can
be added, green herbs, too. Mix with barley
and lentils and let steam covered for last 10
min. of cooking time. (makes about 8 cups)

SWISS-BARLEY BAKE

Have 6 c. cooked barley, about 2 c. cooked in
5 c. water as in basic recipe. Saute 1 lg.
onion or 1 bunch scallions, 1/2 lb. mushrooms
in 2 T. oil for 5 min. Add barley and 3 T. tamari and mix well. Make 2 layers alternating
the barley mixture with 1 lb. grated swiss on
each layer. Bake with a sprinkle of paprika
for 15 min., just until cheese has melted.
(makes 6 servings)

BARLEY

BARLEY BALLS

Follow the recipe for Montezuma rice balls substituting barley for rice. Like the rice, it
is best to have the barley a bit stickier than
you would normally make. Do this by cooking
the barley 60 min. with 4 c. water and no salt.
Any of the variations are equally as good as
with rice. I love them made with barley.

BULGHUR

Bring 2 1/2 c. water to a boil and add 1 c.
bulghur wheat and 2 T. oil. Cook 30 min. and
let sit 10 min. covered. This can also be
roasted before cooking. (makes about 3 or 4
cups)

PEAS AND BULGHUR

Soak 1 c. washed chick peas over night in 3 c.
water. Add 3 c. water and 1 T. oil and bring
to a boil. Cook covered 1 1/2 hours with 2 bay
leaves and 2 T. cumin seed. Add 1 c. bulghur
and cook 30 min. Saute 1 bunch leeks or scallions, 1 red sweet pepper or green in 1 T. oil
for 5 min. Add to bulghur mixture and steam,
covered 10 min. off flame. (serves 6 people)

SESAME-LEMON FRIED BULGHUR

Roast 1/4 c. whole sesame seeds in pan until
brown and crumbly. Add 3 T. oil and 4 c. cooked
bulghur and mix well, cooking until hot. Add
the juice and grated peel of 2 lemons. Tamari
to taste and serve.
Or you may serve with a sauce made from 1 c.
water, 1/4 c. tahini and 1/4 c. tamari, mixed
together and added to mixture before lemon.
(serves 4)

BULGHUR BURGHURS

2 c. cooked bulghur
1/2 c. buckwheat flour
2 T. tahini
1/4 c. oil
1/2 c. diced onions
2 T. tamari

Mix together, adding water, to make a sticky
batter. Heat lightly greased griddle or iron
fry pan and spread by spoonfuls to desired size.
Turn when browned well and brown other side.
Eat them with sauce or plain.
Keep them thin so they cook in the middle easily.

QUINUA (pronounced keen-wah)

This is a very special grain that I have just
found out about. It's from South America,
grown at an altitude of 9,000 feet. It has not
been commercially imported to this country yet,
but in hopes that it soon will, I have included
information for cooking it that I have found
through using it. It is cooked like rice. The
miraculous thing about it is it sprouts as it
cooks, making a very light and low starch
grain. Used for sprouting, it is ready to use
in 2 days. Any way the other grains are used,
quinua can also. I hope we can get it soon in
this country.

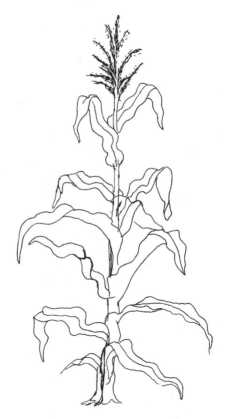

6
BREADS, SPREADS & PASTRIES

BASIC OVERNIGHT BREAD

3 c. cooked grain (rice is always good, but for
  a change, barley is great and so is millet)
1 c. whole wheat flour
1 c. buckwheat flour
2 c. cornmeal
1/4 c. oil
1 rounded t. salt
water

Mix everything but water together until well
blended. Add water until dough is sticky and
feels like patting a fat stomach. Cover and
let sit in warm place overnight. Put in oiled
bread pan and run knife around edges to keep
from sticking. Put in cold oven and turn on to
350°, baking until done through - 1 1/2 hours.
(It should look golden and not feel soft when
pressed on with your fingers). Remove from
pan by hitting end of bread pan flat on hard
surface and turning bread out into other hand.
Cool before cutting. Serve with miso-tahini
spread: walnut-sized piece miso softened with
a little water, about 3 times as much tahini
(it's up to you how strongly miso you want it);
mix together to smooth paste. This is a basic
recipe to which can be added minced onions or
parsley, or garlic, sprouts, grated carrots,
any number of things.

SALT-RISING BREAD

Scald 1 c. milk or nut milk. Add 1 T. honey,
1 1/2 t. salt and 1/4 c. cornmeal. Put in 2
qt. jar and set in pan of hot water (120°) in
a warm place overnight until bubbles rise free-
ly as gas escapes. Stir in 1 c. luke warm water, 1 T. honey, 2 T. oil, 2 c. light whole
wheat flour and beat well. Return to hot water
and let rise until light and full of bubbles.
Put in a large warm mixing bowl and gradually
add enough flour to make a stiff dough. Knead
10-15 min. until smooth. Divide in half and
shape for loaves. Put in oiled pans and let
rise in a warm place until 2 1/2 times the size.
Bake 10 min. at 375° and 25 min. at 350°. Remove from pans after cooling 10 min. and cool
on rack.

KNEAD OVERNIGHT BREAD DOUGH TO A STICKY THICK BATTER.

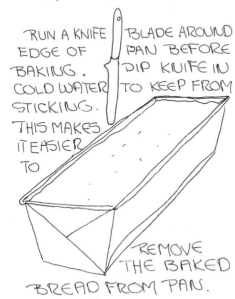

RUN A KNIFE BLADE AROUND EDGE OF PAN BEFORE BAKING. DIP KNIFE IN COLD WATER TO KEEP FROM STICKING. THIS MAKES IT EASIER TO REMOVE THE BAKED BREAD FROM PAN.

ONION BREAD

Add 1 c. of onions sauteed until brown in 1 T. oil to basic recipe. Prepare in the same way.

CORN-RYE BREAD

3 c. corn flour or meal
2 c. rye flour
1 c. buckwheat flour
1 T. caraway seeds, crushed
2 c. oil
2 t. salt
water

Mix ingredients and add enough water to make sticky but firm dough. Knead a bit, then sit in warm place 12-24 hours depending on how sour you like it. Put in cold oven and bake at 350° for 1 1/2 hours, until golden brown and firm. Cool before slicing.

BATTER WHOLE WHEAT BREAD

3 c. water or fresh milk
5-6 c. whole wheat pastry flour
6 T. honey
2 T. yeast or 2 cakes
4 T. oil
1/2 t. salt

Scald milk and cool to luke warm. Add and dissolve yeast in the milk. Honey, salt, and oil can be beaten in and then flour added until dough is soft and sticky. Beat as much as you can. Cover to let rise in warm spot until light and doubled in size. Press down and put in oiled pans, filling half-way. Put in warm place uncovered until risen again. Bake until well browned at 375° for 25-30 min.

HERB BREAD

Make a basic batter whole wheat bread, scalding 1 T. dry parsley, 2 t. chives, 1 t. oregano, 1 t. savory, 1 t. basil, 1 t. fennel seeds in milk or water before cooling and adding yeast. Finish as with the basic recipe.

YEAST

USUALLY FOUND IN GRANULAR, DRY FORM OR FRESH CAKES WHICH SHOULD BE USED

WITHIN A SHORT TIME. ALWAYS REFRIGERATE YEAST TO MAINTAIN BACTERIAL CULTURE AND INSURES LIGHT, WELL RISEN BREAD.

CHEDDAR CHEESE BREAD

1 lb. raw white cheddar
6-7 c. flour (whole wheat pastry)
2 c. fresh milk
4 T. butter or oil
2 T. honey
2 T. yeast
1/2 t. salt
egg (if wanted)

Scald milk and add grated cheese. Cool until warm and dissolve yeast in it. Beat in oil, honey, and salt and add flour to make a soft solid mass which can be kneaded easily. Set in warm place with cover and let rise until double. Knead down and shape into loaves. Put in oiled bread pans or braid dough and bake on tray in 375° oven for 30-35 min., basting a few times with a beaten egg. Cool and serve warm.
Plain or with jam, cream cheese, fresh butter.

BREAD DOUGH KNEADING

I ALWAYS DO MY KNEADING RIGHT IN THE BOWL. THE IDEA IS TO FOLD THE LUMP OF DOUGH OVER AND TO FORCE THE TWO HALVES TOGETHER USING THE HEELS OF YOUR HANDS THIS FOLDING AND PUSHING TOGETHER FORCES AIR POCKETS OUT MAKING A THICK ELASTIC FEELING DOUGH.

HOT CHAPATIS

2 c. cornmeal or flour
2 c. whole wheat pastry flour
1 c. chick pea flour
2 crushed red peppers (hot)
5 cloves, crushed chopped garlic
1 T. cumin seed, crushed
2 T. paprika, ground
1 T. turmeric, ground
1 t. coriander
1/4 t. ground cardamom
1/2 t. ground cayenne seed, crushed
1/2 c. olive oil
2 T. poppy seeds
1/4 c. tamari
8 oz. yoghurt
1 T. caraway seeds, crushed
water (boiling)
arrowroot flour or cornmeal
1 t. each of oregano, basil or mixture

Heat together the seeds, pepper and garlic in oil for a min. Add to flour, along with yoghurt, tamari and herbs. Mix in enough water to make solid workable dough. Roll out little balls of dough on cornmeal until very flat and bake on an ungreased skillet until browned on both sides.
Roll up with butter, ghee, grated cheese, more yoghurt or thick milk.

SESAME CHAPATIS

Mix together 3 c. whole wheat pastry flour, 1 t. salt and 1/2 c. oil. Add enough hot water to make a soft pliable dough. Roll out little balls on sesame seeds and bake in heavy ungreased skillet over med. heat for 10-15 min. (makes 12)

CRACKERS

Follow chapatis recipe but roll into smaller rounds or cut in squares and bake at 350° for 20 min.
Make them without seeds or with another seed.

CHEESE WAFERS

1/2 lb. grated cheese
1/4 lb. butter, sweet
1 1/2 c. whole wheat pastry flour
1/2 t. salt
1/8 t. cayenne pepper

Cream together, softened butter and cheese with salt and pepper. Mix in flour. Shape into a roll and wrap in oiled paper. Chill till cold. Slice thin and bake plain or with nuts on top in 400° oven 10 min. on ungreased cookie sheets.

CRACKERS CAN BE ROLLED OUT AS ONE PIECE AND THE DOUGH CUT WITH COOKIE CUTTERS -- ANY SHAPE.

DECORATE WITH SEEDS, NUTS OR DRY FRUIT.

PANCAKES

2 c. whole wheat flour
1 c. buckwheat flour
5 c. water
6 eggs, separated
1/4 c. oil
2 T. honey
1 t. salt

Mix everything together but egg whites, beat
them until very stiff and turn in. Bake on
heavy ungreased or lightly oiled griddle or
skillet until well browned on each side.
If you want even lighter pancakes, add 1 t.
baking soda to batter.

EGGLESS YEAST PANCAKES

3 c. warm water or scalded milk
1 1/2 c. flour mixture (1 c. whole wheat and
        1/2 c. buckwheat)
2 T. yeast or 2 cakes
4 T. oil or butter
4 T. honey
1/2 t. salt

Mix warm liquid and yeast until blended. Mix
in salt, honey and oil, then flour. Let rise
in warm place until double in size. Stir down
and spoon onto heavy, lightly oiled or ungreased skillet and bake over med. flame.

FRIED BREADS - PURI

1 c. whole wheat pastry flour
1 c. buckwheat flour
1 lg. onion, chopped
1 t. salt
2 T. sesame seeds
2 c. water

Chill well after mixing everything together.
Drop by the spoonful into hot oil (360°).
(makes 1 1/2 doz. little puffed breads)

GREEN LITTLE
LEAVES ON
WOODS'
GROUND
SUMMER AND
WINTER

WINTERGREEN

DONUTS

2 c. fresh raw milk
5 c. whole wheat pastry flour
1/2 c. honey
2 T. yeast
1 T. grated orange peel
1/4 lb. butter
2 t. cinnamon
1/2 t. nutmeg

Scald milk with spices and orange peel. Add
butter, honey and salt. Cool and dissolve
yeast in it. Add flour to make soft workable
dough. Cover and let rise in warm place until
double. Roll out 1/2" thick and cut in donut
shapes. Set on well floured board to rise until double. Drop into 365° oil until golden
brown on each side. Drain and cool.
Dip in honey or maple syrup before cooling.
If you have a donut machine use less flour to
make a sticky, thick batter that will drop
through bottom of machine.

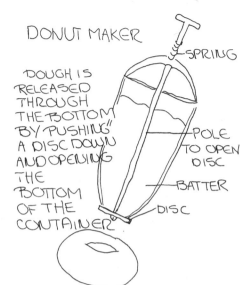

DONUT MAKER

SPRING

DOUGH IS RELEASED THROUGH THE BOTTOM BY "PUSHING" A DISC DOWN AND OPENING THE BOTTOM OF THE CONTAINER

POLE TO OPEN DISC

BATTER

DISC

WHEN THE DISC SPRINGS BACK, IT MAKES THE HOLE IN THE CENTER AS IT CLOSES. THE DONUT MAKER WORKS WITH A WET, THICK AND STICKY BATTER.

SAFFRON FLOWER

FRITTERS

1 c. chopped apple, pineapple, cherries
2 c. whole wheat pastry flour
1/2 c. honey
2 1/2 c. water
1/2 t. salt

Mix up ingredients well and drop by spoonfuls
into hot oil (365°) until well golden brown.
Drain. (makes about 1 doz.)
For lighter fritters, separate 3 eggs. Add
yolks to batter and fold in stiffly beaten
egg whites before frying.

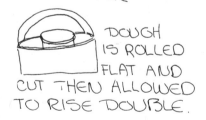

DONUT CUTTER

DOUGH IS ROLLED FLAT AND CUT THEN ALLOWED TO RISE DOUBLE.

STICKY BUNS

ROLL DOUGH WITH SPICE ON IT AND SLICE INTO SWIRLS. SET SIDE-BY-SIDE IN BAKE PAN

KRINGLE

FOLD KRINGLE DOUGH IN THIRDS AND ROLL FLAT. REPEAT AS INSTRUCTED AND SHAPE FOR BAKING AFTER FILLING.

BASIC SWEET YEAST DOUGH

2 c. scalded milk or hot water, cooled to warm
5-6 c. whole wheat pastry flour
1/4 c. butter or oil
3 beaten eggs
2 T. yeast or 2 cakes
1/2 c. honey
1/2 t. salt
1/4 t. vanilla

Dissolve yeast in liquid. Add salt, butter, honey, vanilla and eggs, beat in 1/2 the flour. Mix in flour until dough is easily worked but not sticky. Let rise until double and use in following recipes:

MAPLE STICKY BUNS

One recipe sweet roll dough. After rising, punch down and let rest while you butter or oil a square or round baking pan and pour 2 c. maple syrup in. Sprinkle all over with chopped raw cashews. Roll dough into a rectangle and smear with butter or oil. Sprinkle with cinnamon and maple syrup and roll up into tube. Slice into round cinnamon swirls and lay in pan on maple-nut mixture. Butter or oil well and let rise until light and high. Bake at 375° for 20-25 min. (makes a doz.)

FRUIT AND NUT KRINGLE

1/2 basic recipe
1/2 lb. butter

After dough has risen until double, divide into 2 parts and roll 1 part into a rectangle 1/4" thick. Spread with 2 T. butter and fold in thirds. Roll out again and repeat doing this 3 times with each piece of dough. Chill a bit. Roll into long rectangle and fill down the center. Fold over each side and seal together by pressing with your fingers. Brush with butter and bake at 375° for 20 min. Cool and glaze with a thin dry milk frosting. (makes 2 kringles)

FRUIT-NUT FILLING

4 c. sliced apples or 2 c. apples
2 c. fresh pineapple
1 c. honey
1 c. chopped nuts

Mix together and spread down center of each
kringle and prepare for baking.

POPPY SEED ROLLS

Grind 1 c. poppy seeds and mix with 1/2 c. honey and 4 T. soft butter until you have a paste.
Have basic sweet roll dough ready and roll it
out to a rectangle. Spread with poppy seeds
and roll into a tube. Cut in rounds and lay on
greased sheet. Let rise until double. (makes
a dozen large rolls)
Work butter into dough as with kringle to make
any of the sweet rolls lighter.
Baste with a beaten egg or butter.

COCONUT ROLLS

Work basic dough with butter like kringle. Roll
out 1/4" thick and cut into 3" squares. Spread
with coconut filling and fold in half and seal
ends well. Cut slashes in from fold an inch
long. Fan out the cut sections and let rise
on baking sheets until double. Bake as other
sweet rolls.

COCONUT FILLING

2 c. dry shredded coconut soaked 1-2 hours in
   2 c. fresh cream or 1 1/2 c. whole milk and
   1/4 lb. butter
1/4 lb. butter
1/2 c. honey
1 T. grated orange peel

Mix it together and use to fill coconut rolls.
(1 1/2 dozen big rolls)

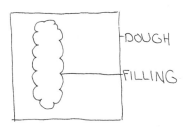

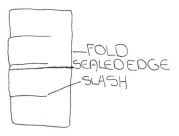

ALMOND ROLLS

Roll out basic recipe dough and cut into big circles (4"-5"). Spread with almond filling and roll up into little cylinders. Seal loose edge and let rise on greased baking sheet until double. Baste with butter and bake at 375° for 20-25 min.

ALMOND FILLING

1 lb. almonds, chopped
1/4 lb. butter, soy butter or almond butter
3/4 c. honey
1/2 t. vanilla extract

After mixing together, spread on dough and bake.

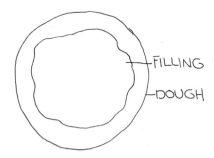

FILLING
DOUGH

ROLL AND SEAL.

SHORTENING BREAD

1 1/2 c. flour
1/4 lb. butter
1/4 c. honey

Cream butter and honey, add flour and mix. Roll out 1/2" thick on floured board. Cut into shapes and bake on lightly greased sheet for 20 min. at 350°.

BANNOCK

This is a hodge-podge bread of anything you have handy. I usually use cornmeal, rolled oats, whole wheat flour, oil, currants, apple slices, cinnamon, nuts or sunflower seeds, honey, molasses, a pinch of salt and baking soda. I grease a big iron skillet, heat it up and pour in the batter. Then I turn the heat down and cook covered 10-15 min. Then I slide it out onto a plate, heat a bit more oil in skillet and pour it over bannock. Turn pan upside down over bannock and turn bannock into skillet. Cook covered another 10-15 min. Cool a bit uncovered and eat pieces plain or with butter or honey.

APPLESAUCE SHORTBREAD

3 c. whole wheat pastry flour
2 c. applesauce
3/4 c. butter or soy butter
1 egg yolk
1 c. chopped nuts
1/4 c. honey
1/2 c. salt

Mix 1/2 the applesauce with everything but the
nuts. Beat until smooth. Spread dough onto a
rectangle and prick with a fork. Bake in 350°
oven for 15 min. and at 300° for 25 min. Cut
and cover with mixture of 1 c. applesauce and
nuts mixed together.

HOMINY BREAD

1 c. cooked cracked corn
1 c. raw cracked corn
1 egg
2 T. oil
1/2 t. salt

Mix cooked corn, oil, egg and salt until smooth.
Add raw corn and bake on sheet or muffin tins
for 30 min. at 350°.

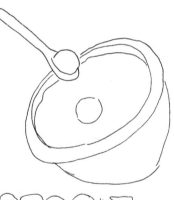

RICE SPOON BREAD

1 c. cooked rice
3 T. cornmeal
1 T. whole wheat flour
1 c. boiling water
1 T. honey
1 c. milk
1 t. salt
1 T. oil
2 eggs, separated

DIP IT OUT HOT FROM
THE OVEN WITH A
WOODEN SPOON.

Mix dry ingredients and honey. Pour in boiling
water and stir until thick. Add rice, oil and
egg yolks beaten with milk. Turn in stiffly
beaten egg whites. Bake in a greased pan set
in a tray of hot water or over a pan of water
at 350° for 35-40 min. Serve right away.

TAHINI-MISO SPREAD

1/2 c. tahini
1/4 c. warm water
a little ball (about 2 T.) miso

Soften miso in water and mix to a smooth paste.
Stir in tahini until smooth and use on bread,
with raw vegetables, or spread it on anything
you want.

TAHINI-MISO SPREAD WITH VEGETABLES

Chop fine and saute or add raw:

2 cloves garlic
1 med. onion
1/2 green pepper
3 stalks parsley
or whatever you like

TAHINI-MISO SPREAD WITH SEEDS

Dry roast until brown and add:

1/3 c. sunflower seeds
1/4 c. sesame seeds
1/3 c. chopped pumpkin seeds

TAHINI-TAMARI SPREAD

1/2 c. tahini
1/4 c. water
4 T. tamari
2 cloves garlic, chopped

Mix together and use the same as miso-tahini
spread.

TAHINI-CUMIN-LEMON

1/2 c. tahini
2 t. ground cumin seed
juice of 2 lemons
1 t. salt

Mix salt, lemon and cumin and add to tahini.
Good on crackers and other bread things.

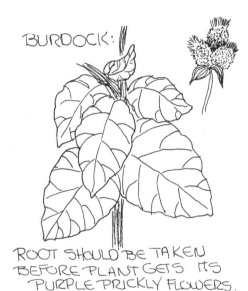

BURDOCK:

ROOT SHOULD BE TAKEN
BEFORE PLANT GETS ITS
PURPLE PRICKLY FLOWERS.

TAHINI-BEAN

Mash up 2 c. of your favorite beans and stir in
1/2 c. tahini, some chopped vegetables and 2 T.
tamari.

TAHINI-CHICKPEA-GARLIC

1/2 c. tahini
1 t. cumin seed
juice of 2 lemons
1 c. chick peas, cooked
2 T. tamari

Mash chick peas and add other ingredients.

BLACK BEAN-ONION

Cook 1 c. beans and 4 c. water (or use 2 1/2 c.
cooked beans), 3 bay leaves, 2 T. oil, 2 T. paprika, 4 cloves garlic for 30 min. before beans
are finished cooking. Let cool a bit while you
chop 3 med. onions into pieces and saute in 1
T. oil until tender and somewhat transparent.
Remove bay leaves from beans and mash well with
a potato masher. Add onions and 3 T. tamari.
Mix well. For breads, crackers, dip for vegetables. (makes about 3 cups spread)

LENTIL-SWEET PEPPER

Cook 1 c. lentils with 3 c. water or stock (or
2 c. cooked lentils) for 1 hour. Add 1 t. basil, 2 t. oregano, 1/2 t. cayenne, 3 T. oil and
1 t. salt. Bubble gently 30 min. more. Cool.
Chop 1 red and 1 green sweet pepper and saute
a short time in 1 T. oil until bright, bright
green. Mash lentils and add to peppers with
1 T. tamari and mix it up. (makes about 3 c.)

CHICK PEA-CARROT-GARLIC

Take 2 c. cooked chick peas and mash. Heat 2 T.
oil and add 1 t. cumin seed and 1 T. paprika.
Stir in 4 cloves chopped garlic, then 2 carrots,
grated or chopped fine. Stir and cover for
5 min. Add 2 T. tamari, chick peas, and mix
well. (3 cups spread)

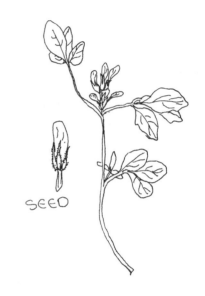

SEED

FENUGREEK
SEED IS USED.
DELICIOUS TEA AND
MAKES GOOD SPROUTS
FOR MIXING IN SALADS,
SOUPS, SPREADS...

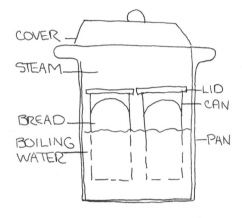

STEAMED BROWN BREAD

3 c. whole wheat pastry flour
1 c. cornmeal
1 c. molasses
1/2 c. honey
1 c. currants
1 c. chopped nuts
4 T. oil
1/2 t. salt
water

Mix together with water to make thick sticky batter and let rise over night. Stir down and half fill greased tall tin cans with batter. Let rise 12-24 hours and steam in boiling water with saucers covering each can and a lid covering entire steaming pot. Takes about 3 hours. Remove bread from cans to cool.
  (2 loaves)

CRANBERRY-NUT BREAD

3 c. whole wheat pastry flour
1 c. cranberries
4 eggs, separated
1 c. honey
1/2 c. chopped nuts
1 c. water
1/2 c. butter or oil
2 T. orange peel
1 t. soda

Cook cranberries, water and honey together until cranberries are tender. Add oil, orange peel and egg yolk and beat together. Mix flour and soda together in bowl, add cranberries and nuts to it. Turn in stiffly beaten egg whites. Bake in 2 small greased bread pans for 40 min. at 350°.

MISO BALLS

1 c. whole wheat pastry flour
1 c. cornmeal
egg-sized lump of miso
1 med. onion, chopped
4 T. oil
1 c. cooked brown rice
3 chopped cloves garlic
1 T. tamari
water

Saute onion in 2 T. oil. Mix all other ingredients and add enough water to make a stiff
dough. Form into little balls with your hands.
Bake on sheet in 350° oven 20-25 min., until
brown.

SOY BUTTER

This is exactly the same as the whipped soy
cream recipe. Boil a couple T. of soy powder
in a c. of water. Stir it a few times (5 min.).
The next part can be done 3 ways. The first way
is using a wire whip (these are great to have
for making sauces and other creamy things).
Pour hot soy water into a bowl and very slowly
pour 2 c. cold-pressed oil (soy, safflower or
corn oil work well). Whip briskly while you
pour, until all the oil is in and mixture is
fluffy like mayonnaise. Add a little salt to
taste if you want. The other methods are (2)
with an egg beater, this way you have to pour
a little oil then beat it in or get a friend
to pour slowly while you beat. The third way
is with a blender, wire whip or beater combination. Pour hot soy water into blender, cap
and turn on high speed. Add herbs or garlic
to soy-water mixture before adding oil. Slowly
pour oil through hole until it gets too thick
for the blender to whip. Have a bowl ready and
pour it in. Finish by beating the rest of the
oil in with the whip or beater. Add salt to
taste or even pinches of some herb you like,
such as parsley, dill, sage, savory, thyme...
or mixtures.

ROSEMARY

LILAC
FLOWERS

7
BEANS

BASIC BEAN RECIPE

Wash and soak 2 c. beans overnight in cold water 3 inches over beans. Drain and cover with fresh cold water, 1 inch. Bring to boil. Add 2 T. oil and simmer covered 1 1/2 hours. Some of the fast cooking beans will be done sooner. Green lentils can be eaten in an hour of cooking and Syrian lentils will take only 30-45 minutes. Some may take longer: chickpeas 2 hours, soy beans 2-3 hours. After 1 1/2 hours (or 30 minutes before beans are cooked) add 1 t. salt and cook 30 minutes more.

Optional: Add herbs with salt, 2 T. crushed cumin, 3 bay leaves, 1 t. oregano, 1/2 t. cayenne, 2 T. paprika.

BEANS

BEST COOKED IN A CLAY POT, BUT IF YOU DON'T HAVE ONE, A HEAVY METAL POT IS FINE.

ADUKI BEANS WITH ONIONS

Use basic recipe. When aduki beans have cooked 1 1/2 hours add 2 lg. onions. Chop and saute 5 minutes in 2 T. oil, 1 t. salt, and 1 T. tamari. Cook 20 minutes more.

ADUKI BURGERS

2 c. cooked aduki beans
1 c. corn meal
1 c. buckwheat flour
3 T. tamari
3 crushed cloves garlic
1 lg. chopped onion
  water

Make thick batter of ingredients. Spread in patty shapes on heavy ungreased or lightly greased skillet. Heat over medium flame until well browned on both sides. Use alone or on sandwiches. Melt cheese on top if desired.
  (makes approx. 18 burgers)

ADUKI RICE

Cook 1 c. aduki beans and 1 T. oil in 4 c. water
for 1 hour. Add 2 c. rice and 4 c. of cold
water. Bring to a boil and cook for 40 min.,
covered. Turn off for 10 min. (serves 6)

CHICKPEAS-CARROTS-ONIONS

2 c. cooked chickpeas
3 chopped carrots
1 lg. onion
2 T. tamari
2 T. oil

Heat oil and saute onion for 1 min. Add carrot and chickpeas and simmer together 10 min.
Add tamari and eat. (serves 6)

COLD ONION-DILL CHICKPEAS

4 c. cold cooked chickpeas
1 bunch scallions or 4 sm. mild onions
2 T. dillweed
1/4 c. oil
Juice of 3 lemons
1 t. salt

Slice onions into little rings. Mix everything
together and let chill at least an hour so the
flavors blend. (serves 6)
Try adding 2 T. tahini and 2 cloves garlic to
recipe.

CHICKPEAS AND GRAVY

When 2 c. chickpeas are almost cooked, add 1/4 c.
tahini and 2 T. tamari. Cook 30 min. over low
flame and stir. Makes a nice light gravy.
Add tomatoes, onions, garlic, mushrooms.

ADUKI BEANS
TINY DARK RED BEANS WITH A SHORT WHITE LINE ON EACH. ANOTHER MEMBER OF THE SOY FAMILY.

CHICK PEAS
ARE NATIVE TO THE MIDDLE EAST, BUT ARE INCLUDED IN THE MAIN FOODS OF COUNTRIES NORTH AND SOUTH. IT'S A ROUND, LIGHT PINK LEGUME A BIT BIGGER THAN A GREEN PEA.

BLACK BEAN STEW

Black beans can be so delicious if cooked cor-
rectly. Using 2 c. beans, make the basic bean
recipe. (This is a bean that cooks better when
soaked overnight). In 2 T. oil saute 1 lg.
onion, 1 section of lotus root chopped small
(if you can get it), 2 med. parsnips, 2 big
turnips, 2 carrots, 2 T. caraway seeds, and 2
stalks celery for a few min. each. Add to beans
and cook together over med. flame for 20 min.
   (serves 6)
Topped with sour cream or yoghurt, this is
great!

BLACK BEAN

MEMBER OF SOY FAMILY.
BLACK WITH WHITE LINE
ON ONE SIDE

LENTIL-CORN BURGERS

2 c. cooked dark lentils
1 c. whole wheat pastry flour
2 c. corn meal
1 c. corn (if possible)
1 chopped onion
2 cloves chopped garlic
2 T. oil
1 t. salt

Mix together into a thick sticky batter (use
water if necessary.) Make patties and heat
over med. flame on greased or ungreased skillet until well browned on both sides. Either
way works fine. (approx. 15 burgers)

CELERY AND LENTILS

This is simple and so good. Cook 2 c. lentils
as with basic recipe. Chop 1 whole bunch celery, tops and all, and a med. size onion and
saute in 2 T. oil for 2 or 3 min. Add to
lentils and saute together for 20 min. Stir
in 1 t. salt. (serves 4)

SPICY SYRIAN LENTILS   (The Little Orange Ones)

Heat 2 T. oil and add 3 cloves chopped garlic,
1 T. curry powder, 2 T. paprika, 2 t. cumin
seed, and 1 fresh red hot pepper or 2 t. cayenne. Add to 2 c. Syrian lentils which have
been cooked by basic recipe 25 min. Cook together 20 min. more. (6 med. portions)

MUNG BEANS AND RICE   (Another Spicy One)

Cook 2 c. soaked mung beans in water (covered
3 in.) for 1 hour. Add 3 c. of rice and make
sure water is 1 1/2"-2" over beans and rice.
Add some if not. Cook 1 hour together stirring
occasionally. Saute 5 cloves garlic, 2 T.
turmeric, 1 t. crushed coriander and 1 t. caraway seeds, and 1/4 t. crushed cardamom, 2 T.
paprika, 2 hot peppers or 1 T. cayenne, Add
this to rice and beans along with 1 t. salt
and cook another 20 min. Add 1/2 c. ghee
(clarified butter) and 1 T. tamari right at
the end. (makes a pot big enough for a dozen)
If you add chopped vegetables with the spices,
you can make enough for a few more. Also try
melted cheese in it.

LENTILS

FLAT, ROUND AND GREEN
OR RED (SYRIAN). FAST
COOKING BEAN.

PINTO CHILE

Cook 2 c. pinto beans, 2 t. cayenne, 1 T. cumin
seed and 2 T. oil like basic recipe for 1 1/2
hours. Saute 2 stalks celery, 1 large onion,
1 sweet pepper, 1 hot red pepper (or 1 T. chile
powder), 1 T. paprika and 2 lb. ripe tomatoes
in 2 T. oil for a few min. Add to beans and
cook together 20 min. Eat in bowls like soup
or pour on rice. (enough for 6)

REFRIED BEANS

4 c. cooked pintos
2 lg. onions
3 chopped cloves garlic
1 t. cayenne
2 t. oregano
1 t. cumin seed
2 T. oil

Saute onions, garlic and herbs until onions
are just tender. Add cooked pintos and mash
with a potato masher or fork. Cook until hot
and add 1 t. salt.
Butter or ghee added with the salt is good too!

SOY BEANS

ARE ONE OF THE MOST
COMPLETE VEGETABLE
SOURCES OF PROTEIN.
IT IS ALSO ONE OF THE
HARDEST FOODS TO
DIGEST AND MUST BE
THOROUGHLY COOKED
BEFORE EATING. I HAVE
FOUND THAT MASHED OR
GROUND BEANS ARE
EASIER ON DIGESTION
THAN THE WHOLE BEAN.

SOY MILK (With A Blender)

Let 3 c. soy beans soak in 5 c. cold water 1-2
days. Wash 1 or 2 times a day. Put a bit at
a time in the blender adding 2 c. water to 1 c.
soy beans. Blend just a few seconds (10-15)
and strain through cheese cloth. Do all the
soy beans the same way. Put the liquid on a
med. flame and cook to a boil stirring often.
Cook at a slow boil 10 min. stirring often.
When done, let cook and put in bottles to be
kept cold until used. (makes about 2 quarts
milk)

SOY MILK (Without A Blender)

1 c. soy flour
2 qts. cold water

Mix 1/2 the water with the soy flour. Add in
the rest of the water. Bring to a boil, stirring often; bubble gently for 20 min., still
stirring often (a double boiler is even better.)
Strain through cheese cloth and keep cold until
used.

SOY BURGERS

You should have pulp left over when you strain
soy milk from whole soy beans. To this pulp
add 3 crushed cloves garlic, 1 lg. chopped
onion, 1 t. oregano, 1 t. salt, 1 t. savory,
2 T. oil and enough flour to make a thick,
sticky dough. Make burger patties. Using
either greased or ungreased heavy skillet, heat
burgers over med. flame until well browned on
both sides.
If you don't have pulp from soy milk, mash up
3 c. cooked soy beans and use instead.

BAKED BEANS

Cook 5 lb. soy beans using basic recipe. After
beans have cooked 1 1/2 hours add to it 5
cloves crushed garlic, 4 bay leaves, a pinch
or two of thyme or rosemary, and 2 T. paprika.
Cook together another 1/2 hour. Then add 4 c.
cut stewed or fresh tomatoes, 1/4 c. honey, 2 T.
molasses, 1 chopped green pepper, 3 lg. onions,
1/2 c. cider vinegar, 3 t. salt, 1/4 c. oil,
and 2 T. tamari. Pour into lg. baking pan or
roaster pan and bake at 325° for 1-1 1/2 hours,
until juice is almost absorbed and top is
browned.
Add 4 c. tofu (bean cakes) to mixture before
baking. Sprinkle with well toasted sesame
seeds.

SOY LOAF

4 c. cooked soy beans
2 c. corn meal
1 c. stewed tomatoes
1 chopped carrot
1 lg. chopped onion
1 stalk celery
2 T. tamari
1/2 t. cayenne
1/2 t. basil
1 t. savory
1/4 c. oil

Slightly mash 4 c. cooked soy beans with all ingredients. Mix together into thick dough. Put in greased bread pan and bake at 350° for 1 1/2 hours. Cool and slice. (makes 1 lg. or 2 sm. loaves)
Top with cheese for the last 15 min. of baking.

TOFU

COMMERCIAL TOFU IS USUALLY MADE USING EPSOM SALT (MAGNESIUM SULFATE) AS A COAGULATE.

FOR SOFTER AND SMOOTHER COAGULATION, CALCIUM SULFATE, ANOTHER MINERAL SALT CAN BE USED.

TOFU   (Chinese Soy Bean Cakes)

Make soy milk from 1 of the basic recipes. When the milk has boiled gently for 10-20 min., turn off and add 2 T. epsom salt. Stir it in with as few strokes as possible so curd doesn't get broken and lumpy. Let sit until cooled. Into a colander lined with cheese cloth, gently pour the soy bean curd. Drain liquid into a bowl. Sit a weight on solid curd to squeeze out liquid for a firm cheese. Allow to set until completely cooled. Cut and put in cold water in refrigerator. If left at room temperature, change water 1-2 times a day. If you ever decide to freeze tofu, make sure you drain it well first or else it will be like a sponge when it thaws.

LIMA BEAN

8
SAUCES

BASIC WHITE SAUCE

3/4 c. whole wheat pastry flour, oat, rice or
    barley
1/2 c. oil
2 T. tamari

Heat oil in pan. Add flour and smooth to paste.
Slowly add water (1 quart) and stir until thick.
If you add boiling water to the flour paste,
you won't have to stand around the pot as long.
Add salt or gomasio and tamari to taste.
For a nuttier and darker sauce, dry roast the
flour and add the oil to it. Then finish as
with the basic sauce.

BROWN SAUCE

Follow recipe for white sauce, roasting the
flour and using vegetable stock instead of
water. Flavor with 3 T. tamari (no salt.)

BUCKWHEAT-MUSHROOM GRAVY

Heat 2 T. oil and toss in 1 chopped med. onion.
After 1 or 2 min. of stirring add 1/2 lb.
sliced mushrooms (caps and stems.) Stir a
min. over med. high heat and put in serving
bowl. Follow the recipe for brown sauce using
3/4 c. raw buckwheat flour in place of the
other. Use the same cooking pan as you used
for the mushrooms. When sauce is thick, add
mushrooms and mix. Simmer 5 min. This is
good on anything too, especially grain burgers
of some kind.

SESAME SAUCE

Roast 1/2 c. unhulled sesame seeds in pan until
well browned and crumble easily between the
fingers. Add 1/2 c. oil and 3 c. flour. Pro-
ceed as with basic white sauce or roast flour
a bit with seeds, add oil. Then follow the
white sauce recipe. (Try black sesame seeds,
too.)

WIRE WHISK

PERFECT TOOL FOR MAKING
SMOOTH SAUCES

SESAME-CARROT SAUCE

Saute 1 med. chopped onion in 2 T. oil for a
min. Add chopped carrot, stir a min. Cover
and let cook about 5 min. until carrot is just
tender. Remove and put in bowl. Put 1/4 c.
sesame seeds in pan and roast well. Add the
flour and roast it, then the oil. Follow the
basic recipe and when thick add the carrots.
Simmer for 5 min. A fine grain or noodle
sauce. I even used to eat this sauce like soup.

CHICK PEA-SQUASH SAUCE

Heat 2 T. oil in wok or pan and add 1 sm.
chopped onion and 1 c. butternut squash in
small pieces. Stir. Cook until just tender
over med. heat with lid on. Add chick peas and
1/2 t. basil and 1/2 t. savory or your favorite herbs. Toss together and cover again,
cooking 5 min. Remove to serving bowl. In
the same pan make the white sauce (roasted or
otherwise) and when sauce has thickened add
2 T. tamari and vegetables. Simmer together
for 5 min. Use it on rice or any grain, on
dumplings or noodles.

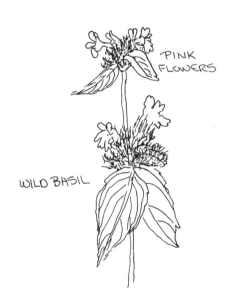

PINK FLOWERS

WILD BASIL

CURRY SAUCE AND FLOUR

Heat 2 T. curry powder, 1/8-1/4 t. of cayenne
(you decide), 2 T. paprika in 1/4 c. oil for
a min. Add another 1/4 c. of oil and 3/4 c.
flour and follow the white sauce recipe. Then
add 1 t. oregano, 1/2 t. basil and 1/4 c.
parsley (fresh) or 2 T. dry. Simmer covered
for 5 min. Add 3 T. tamari and eat. Great
on bulghur and cous-cous.

NUT MILK CREAMY SAUCE

Follow the basic white sauce recipe or any
variation, substituting the 4 c. of water with
4 c. almond, cashew, sunflower or sesame milk
or soy milk, too.

MISO SAUCE #1 (Heavy Cold Weather Sauce)

Make either a basic tahini-onion sauce or white or brown sauce with onions. When thick, turn off the heat. Cool a bit and add an egg size lump of miso, softened in warm water. Beat sauce smooth with a wire whip. Good on vegetables, grain, grain-burgers.

MISO SAUCE #2

egg size lump of miso
1/3 c. flour
3 c. stock
1/3 c. oil
1 lg. onion

Chop and saute 1 lg. onion in 1 T. oil until tender. Soften miso in 1/3 c. warm water. Roast flour until brown and add oil to make thick paste. Slowly add boiling stock and stir until thick and smooth. Turn off heat and add miso.
For a creamier flavor, add 2 T. tahini with the miso.

TOMATO SAUCE

4 lbs. tomatoes, chopped
2 lg. onions
1 green pepper
3 cloves garlic
2-3 bay leaves
2 T. olive oil
2 T. paprika
2 T. tamari
2 t. oregano
1 t. basil
1/2 t. marjoram

Heat paprika and garlic in oil for a min. Add onion, then pepper and tomatoes. Simmer together covered 20 min. Add herbs and simmer 5 min. more. Add tamari to taste. (makes 5-6 cups sauce)
The longer it cooks, the thicker it gets.

CURRY-TOMATO SAUCE

2 lbs. tomatoes
2 c. stock or water
1/2 green pepper
3 cloves garlic, crushed
6 T. oil
6 T. flour
2 T. tamari
2 T. curry powder
1/2 t. basil
1 t. oregano
1 t. cayenne

Heat curry and cayenne in oil for a min. Add
garlic and flour. Smooth in water. Add
chopped tomato and pepper and stir until hot
and thick. Sprinkle in herbs and bubble gently for 5 min. Add tamari to taste and serve
on grain, vegetables, noodles. (5-6 cups sauce)

GINGER-VEGETABLE SAUCE

2 tomatoes
1 carrot
2 stalks celery
1 lg. onion
1 clove garlic
1/2 sweet red pepper
4 c. water
1/2 c. arrowroot flour or starch
2-3 leaves each of either kale, chard, spinach,
    turnips, chopped (or whatever greens are
    available)
2 t. grated fresh ginger
3 T. tamari
2 T. oil

Saute garlic and onion a min. in oil, add ginger and carrot. Cover 5 min. Add celery, pepper and tomatoes with boiling water. Stir in
the arrowroot softened in cold water and continue to stir until thick and clear. Add
greens and tamari. (6-7 cups sauce)

WILD GINGER: FOUND IN RICH
WOODLAND SOIL. MUCH SMALLER
ROOT THAN CULTIVATED
GINGER WHICH IS
USUALLY FOUND
IN KITCHENS.

THE FOLEY FOOD MILL

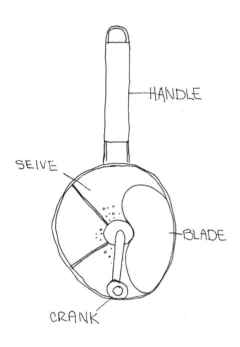

HANDLE

SEIVE

BLADE

CRANK

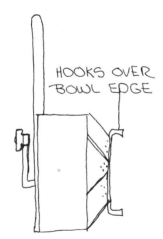

HOOKS OVER
BOWL EDGE

PUMPKIN SAUCE

Cut open a pumpkin, take out the seeds, and
slice in pieces. Steam in water 15 min. Puree
with water in blender or Foley food mill. Saute   slices of 1 lg. onion in 1 T. oil until
tender. Add pumpkin puree and heat. Add ta-
mari to taste. (6-8 cups sauce)
Creamy with 4 T. tahini.

BARBEQUE SAUCE

1 lg. onion
2 stalks celery
2 crushed cloves garlic
1 c. tomatoes, pureed
1/2 c. raisins
1/2 c. water
1/2 green pepper, chopped
1/2 t. each cayenne, paprika and salt
2 T. oil

Saute the vegetables with the spices. Add
tomato, water and raisins. Simmer 15 min. Add
salt. (2 1/2-3 cups sauce)

TAHINI SAUCE WITH ONIONS

6 c. water
3 med. onions, chopped finely
1 c. tahini
1/4 c. tamari

Sautee onions in oil for 2 min. Add 2 c. water
and tahini and stir until smooth. Gradually
add remaining 4 c. water and stir until sauce
heats and becomes thick. Turn off fire and
add tamari to taste.

TAHINI-TOMATO SAUCE

Follow the directions for tahini onion sauce.
When sauce has thickened add 2 c. of stewed
chopped tomatoes or 2 c. of tomato puree or 1
of each. Salt to taste.

ONION-ARROWROOT SAUCE   (A Clear Brown Gravy)

2 lg. onion, chopped
4 c. stock or water
1/3 c. arrowroot starch or flour
4 T. sesame seeds
2 T. oil
tamari

Roast sesame seeds until brown and crumbly,
add oil and onion. Saute until onion is golden brown. Add boiling stock and arrowroot
which has been softened with 1/3 c. water.
Stir until thickened. Add tamari and pour over
grain, dumplings, noodles. (5-6 cups sauce)
Add 1/2 lb. mushrooms to onions when they're
almost cooked, following the rest of the recipe. Some people like this with lemon juice
in it, and sometimes it's good as a soup. If
you want it thicker, add more arrowroot.

SWEET AND SOUR SAUCE

1 lg. onion, chopped
1 lg. carrot, chopped
3 stalks celery, chopped
1/2 green pepper, chopped
1/4 lb. currants
2 lemons (juice)
1/3 c. arrowroot flour or starch
4 c. apple juice or 3 c. water, 1 c. apple
     concentrate
2 T. paprika
2 T. tamari
1 T. oil

Saute chopped vegetables - onion, carrot, pepper and celery with the paprika and currants
for 10 min. Heat apple juice and add arrowroot mixed smooth in cold water. Stir until
thick and clear. Add lemon and tamari to
taste. (5-6 cups sauce)

ORANGE SAUCE   (Sauce for Sweet Things)

2 c. fresh orange juice
4 T. honey
1/4 c. arrowroot starch or flour
1 t. cinnamon

Mix arrowroot in cold orange juice. Heat,
stirring with cinnamon and honey until thick
and clear.
This is good on pancakes, toast, hot buns.
Good in yoghurt or on fruit salads. Use as
cake filling.

TWO-CHEESE SAUCE

1 lb. sharp, raw cheddar
1 lb. fresh cottage cheese
3 c. raw milk
6 T. oat or whole wheat pastry flour
6 T. oil or butter
1 t. salt

Make a paste from the butter and flour. Slowly
add milk then the cheese, mixing with wire
whisk until thick and smooth. Sprinkle in salt
and eat over bread, whole grains, vegetables.
(6 cups sauce)

YOGHURT-CURRY SAUCE

1 qt. yoghurt
1 c. stock or water
3 stalks fresh parsley or 2 T. dry
2 cloves garlic, crushed
2 T. curry powder
2 T. tamari
2 T. oil

Heat curry in oil for a min. or 2. Add garlic,
oregano and parsley for 5 min, then water and
gradually stir in yoghurt and heat to eating
temperature. Add tamari and pour onto vegetables or add sauteed vegetables and serve on
rice. (makes 4-5 cups sauce)

THANK YOU
FOR THE AIR SO SWEET
THANK YOU
FOR THE FOOD WE EAT
THANK YOU
FOR THE BIRDS THAT SING
THANK YOU
GOD
FOR EVERYTHING.

9
SEAWEED

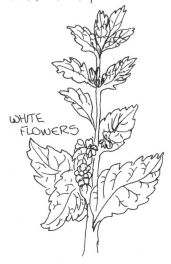

LEMON BALM

WHITE
FLOWERS

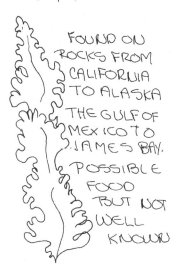

SEA LETTUCE

FOUND ON
ROCKS FROM
CALIFORNIA
TO ALASKA
THE GULF OF
MEXICO TO
JAMES BAY.
POSSIBLE
FOOD
BUT NOT
WELL
KNOWN

HIZIKI

Wash a 3 1/2 oz. pkg. of dry hiziki. Cover with
cold water and soak for 25-30 min. Drain off
water and save to use for cooking grains, soups,
and sauces. Heat 2 T. oil and add hiziki. Stir
a few min., cover and cook over med. flame for
30-45 min. Add 1-2 T. tamari, stir and eat.
Saute a lg. onion with the hiziki.

HIZIKI-CARROTS-ONIONS

Soak and drain a 3 1/2 oz. package of hiziki.
Heat 2 T. oil and add to it 1 lg. onion and 3
carrots, sliced. Stir a min. Add hiziki,
stir together and cook covered over med. flame
for 30-40 min. Add 2 T. tamari and serve.
(vegetable for 6)

HIZIKI RICE

4 c. cooked rice
2 T. oil
1 pkg. cooked hiziki
2 T. tamari
juice of 2 lemons

Heat oil and mix rice and seaweed together until hot. Add lemon and tamari. (enough for 4)

HIZIKI AND TOFU

Soak and drain hiziki. Heat 2 T. oil and add
2 c. tofu and 1 lg. onion. Stir a min. and add
hiziki. Mix, cover and cook over med. heat for
35 min. Add 2 T. tamari and serve.
(enough for 6)
Or: Mix tofu and onion together in the heated
oil. Add hiziki and tamari. Stir and put in
oiled bake pan. Sprinkle with roasted sesame
seeds and bake in 350° oven for 30 min.

HIZIKI-GINGER-LEMON

Soak and drain seaweed. Heat 2 T. oil and add
2 T. of grated fresh ginger, 1 T. ginger powder and seaweed. Stir together and cover, cook
25 min. Add juice of 3 lemons and 2 T. tamari.
(6-8 portions)

HIZIKI SANDWICH

3 c. cooked hiziki
3 c. alfalfa sprouts
tahini-tamari spread with scallions
12 slices bread

Toast the bread and spread all 12 slices. Put
1/2 c. seaweed and 1/2 c. alfalfa sprouts on
each of 6 slices. Lay bread on and slice.
Add tomato, onion, cheese, cucumber, lettuce.
Melt cheese over open face sandwiches.

WAKAME

Wakame, like hiziki, must be well washed but
soaked only 10 min. Drain, saving water for
cooking, and chop wakame into bite size pieces.
Cook 3.5 oz. pkg. alone or with a chopped onion
in 2 T. oil for a few min., stirring. Add a
bit of liquid and cover to cook 10-15 min.

WAKAME IN SOUP

Add wakame, soaked and cut, to any soup along
with vegetables. Use the drained soaking water
as part of soup stock.

WAKAME-SPROUTS-CARROTS

Heat 2 T. oil and add 2 cloves chopped garlic
and 1 lg. onion. Saute a min. and add carrot.
Stir in wakame, soaked and cut. Add a bit of
liquid, cover, and cook 15 min. over med. flame.
Mix in 2 T. tamari and 3 c. sprouts (alfalfa,
mung or mixed). Serve hot with lemon over it,
or lemon and oil mixture.

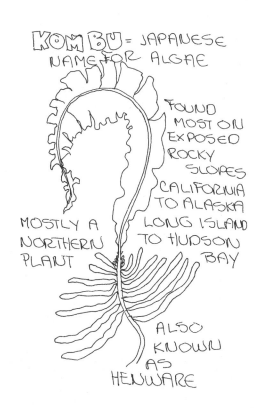

KOMBU = JAPANESE NAME FOR ALGAE

FOUND MOST ON EXPOSED ROCKY SLOPES CALIFORNIA TO ALASKA LONG ISLAND TO HUDSON BAY

MOSTLY A NORTHERN PLANT

ALSO KNOWN AS HENWARE

WAKAME-TAHINI CASSEROLE

Mix 1 pkg. of soaked, drained, and cut wakame
with 1/4 c. tahini, 2 T. tamari, 2 lg. sliced
onions, and 2 c. soaked water. Put in greased
dish and bake at 375° for 25 min.
(enough for 4)

KOMBU

Kombu is a bit tougher to deal with but worth
it. Kombu comes in large leaves which should
be washed and soaked 30 min. Drain, saving
water, and cut into eating pieces. Heat a
little oil and drop drained kombu in. Stir
a min. and add back almost all soaking liquid.
Cover and boil gently 1 1/2-2 hours until kombu
is tender. Add tamari and eat plain or use in
recipes.

FRIED KOMBU

Soak, cut, and drain off all the water from a
pkg. of kombu. Heat deep oil to 360° and drop
in a part of the kombu. Fry until puffed up
and crispy, then drain. Do the rest of the
kombu the same way and cool. Eat like chips.

FRIED KOMBU IN CLEAR BROTH

Fry kombu following the above recipe. Make a
broth from kombu soaking water, 2 lg. sauteed
onions and 2 T. tamari. Pour hot broth in
bowls and float kombu on top.

CREAMED KOMBU

Drain cooked kombu recipe, saving juice for
soup stock. Add 2 chopped onions and kombu to
3 c. thin white sauce. Mix with 3 T. tamari
and bake 25 min. at 350° (enough for 6-8)
Sprinkle with roasted sesame seeds before baking.
Creamed kombu can also be made by following the
wakame-tahini recipe and substituting kombu
instead of wakame.

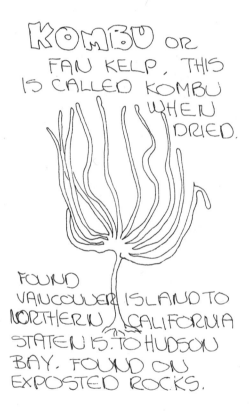

KOMBU OR FAN KELP, THIS IS CALLED KOMBU WHEN DRIED.

FOUND VANCOUVER ISLAND TO NORTHERN CALIFORNIA STATEN IS. TO HUDSON BAY. FOUND ON EXPOSED ROCKS.

NORI-RICE ROLLS

Use the same filling as nori tempura. Roll un-
toasted nori with rice inside, tucking in one
end. Put on greased sheet and bake at 400°
for 20-25 min. Cool slightly and eat.

NORI-SPROUT SANDWICH

For every sandwich you need 1 sheet toasted nori, garlic spread, 1/2 c. alfalfa sprouts, a
big slice of cheese and a thin slice of onion.
Put spread on 1 pc. bread, put on cheese, onion, toasted nori, and sprouts. Spread second
slice of bread and put on top. Put in 400°
oven and toast 5 min. on each side.

NORI TEMPURA

4 c. cooked rice
1/2 c. currants
2 T. tamari
2 T. oil
1/2 c. each finely chopped carrot, onion, celery
1/4 c. sesame seeds
whole wheat tempura batter

Roast seeds brown and add oil. Saute vegetables
and currants a few min. Add rice and tamari
and stir until warm. Roll toasted nori into
long roll with rice inside. Leave ends open,
and cut into 4 pieces. Dip each piece in tempura batter and fry in 360° oil until golden
brown. (makes 30-40 pieces)
Dip in ginger-tamari sauce.

TOASTED NORI

One way to eat nori is to toast it by holding
sheets over a med. flame until entire sheet
becomes bright green. You can eat them like
that or crumble up as a garnish on casserole,
vegetables, sandwiches. I like to crumble it
into my gomasio (sesame salt).

NORI OR LAVER
GROWS NEW JERSEY TO
HUDSON BAY AND
NEW FOUNDLAND.

IT IS SOLD IN
SQUARE SHEETS
USUALLY 10 TO
A PACKAGE AND
IS USED FOR
ROLLING AROUND
RICE, VEGETABLES
OR A FAVORITE
FILLING. NORI CAN
BE TOASTED UNTIL
BRIGHT GREEN
OVER A FLAME
AND FILLED WITH
HOT STUFFING TO
BE EATEN HOT
OR COLD FOR
LATER; OR THE
FILLING CAN BE
ROLLED INSIDE
THE NORI AND
BOTH CAN BE
BAKED TOGETHER.

10
DAIRY

RAW MILK

Raw milk is unheated and in fact, untouched by any processing devices. The cream always separates from the whole milk. When cream is skimmed off, real skimmed milk is left. It is not the same as commercial skimmed milk which has had fat molecules removed from the milk by a machine, leaving a fat free and hard to digest liquid.
Goat's milk is my favorite. We have 4 milk goats on the farm and make our own yoghurt and cheese.

CLABBERED MILK (Cow)

Skim cream off the top of milk, you can get a pint or more from a gallon, and set aside for butter, sour cream, whipped cream or cream cheese. Set skimmed milk in covered pan for 1-2 days, depending on how cold it is, it can take even longer. Milk will get thick like yoghurt and can be used the same ways as yoghurt, but no culture or temperature hassels to go through.

COTTAGE CHEESE (Cow or Goat)

Put clabbered milk in enamel or stainless pan. Heat very, very slowly, uncovered, in oven or on top of double boiler over water. Heat for an hour or more depending on how solid you want the curd, longer it cooks, the harder it is. Turn off heat and let cool. Strain in cheese cloth until whey drips out. (Save whey for making whey cheese, salad dressings, sauces, soups, cooking grains in, vegetables, breads, as a substitute for water). Put curd in bowl and break up with a fork. Eat it dry, with salt or add cream for creamed cottage cheese.

CREAM CHEESE

Put sour cream in pan and heat like cottage cheese. Strain and whip it smooth with a fork. Herbs are good in it, chives, savory, chervil, basil, dill, etc.

BUTTER (Cow or Goat)

This is done without a churn. Put cream in a
jar (half-full) and shake until butter forms on
top of liquid in little yellow lumps. Strain
through cheese cloth and save buttermilk for
drinking or cooking. If you like salted butter,
sprinkle it with sea salt and mix in or add a
pinch or 2 of sea salt before shaking.

GHEE

Bring butter to a slow boil and hold there until
foam is cooked off or skimmed off. Pour clear
yellow ghee into a container and use white milky
fat for cooking with beans, give it to the cat,
or composte it. Some people think it's not good
to eat, suit yourself. The clear butter will
harden when cooled.

SOUR CREAM (Best with Cow's Milk)

Let cream sit out in warm place until it sours
and thickens. It won't be as solid a mass as
commercial sour cream because it's not cultured
like store bought kinds.

YOGHURT

Everyone has to find the warm place in the house
to make yoghurt. Heat 1 qt. raw milk to scalding temperature then cool to 110°. Add 1/2 c.
yoghurt to it and stir well. Cover and keep
in very warm place until it thickens, overnight
is usually perfect. I like doing yoghurt in a
stone crock, it holds temperatures well. The
culture for your next batch of yoghurt can be
taken from the fresh made yoghurt before it is
eaten.
Although the milk is heated, killing enzymes
for digestion, equally beneficial enzymes and
more are replaced in the yoghurt. It's a nu-
tritious, protein food which is good plain,
with honey, with dry fruit, jams and preserves,
on salads, vegetables, you name it.

SALSIFY
(YELLOW GOAT'S BEARD)
PURPLE OR YELLOW
FLOWERED PLANT
FOUND IN NORTH
AMERICA BUT FROM
SOUTHERN EUROPE.

ROOT OF PLANT IS
USED AS A VEGETABLE
SOMETIMES CALLED
OYSTER PLANT.
LOOKS A BIT LIKE
A PARSNIP - FLAVOR
IS NOT THE SAME,
HOWEVER.

CROCK CHEESE (Goat or Cow)

Get an earthen crock, large or small, depending on how much raw milk you have to use. In a lg. jar (2 qts.) put raw milk (if you want to do a smaller batch for the first time, start with a quart or less). Let it get thick and clabbered. Goat's milk curd will separate from the whey and float. Put thick milk in top of double boiler and heat as slowly as possible until milk reaches about 110-130° (should take 45-60 min.). The whey should be at bottom of pan. Let it cool and strain through about 4 layers of cheese cloth until thoroughly drained and then some. Press it into an earthen ware crock, or large cup or deep bowl. Salt the top and cover. Repeat this procedure every other day, pressing cheese together until crock is almost full. If you start clabbering a new batch of milk on the days you make cheese it will be ready on the next cheese day. In hot weather it may only take a day to get thick. When crock is almost full with alternate cheese-salt layers, let it sit a day. Then remove and shape into balls or flat, round pieces. Set out on a board to dry, covered with a dry piece of cheese cloth. Turn once or twice a day for 2-3 days. Wrap up and keep cold for eating. To keep it a long time, put it in a salt and water brine, pretty salty. If it is too salty for your taste, put it in cold fresh water an hour or less before eating it, and salt will be drawn out.

EASTER CHEESE

4 c. fresh raw milk
2 c. butter milk or clabbered milk
4 eggs
1 t. salt
1 t. honey

Scald milk, beat eggs till foamy and add butter milk, salt, and honey. Beat again. Pour mixture into hot sweet milk. Cover and set 15 min. then stir till it separates. Allow to cool. Drain through cheese cloth layed in colander. Set in mold or bowl.

11
NOODLES

NO-EGG NOODLES

2 c. flour
4 T. oil or soy butter
1/2 t. salt
boiling water

Work oil into salt and flour. Add just enough
water to make a solid but pliable dough. Roll
out on floured board and cut into shapes you
want. Cover with a cloth, allow to dry 3-5
days for storage or cook when fresh in boiling,
salted water with a bit of oil for 3-5 min.
Drain and serve with your favorite sauce or
vegetable.

EGG NOODLES

2 c. flour
3 eggs
4 T. oil
1/2 t. salt
boiling water

Mix flour, salt and oil together in large bowl
or on board. Make a pocket in center. Fold
flour into eggs until moist and pliable. If
3 eggs are not enough liquid to get a workable
dough, drops of water should be added. When
soft and smooth, roll dough out on floured surface to desired thickness and cut out shapes.
Dry covered 2-3 days for storage, then seal in
glass jars or container.
There are many ingredients to use in noodles,
with or without egg, add:

WHOLE WHEAT: Use 2 c. whole wheat pastry flour
for either of the basic recipes.

BUCKWHEAT: 1 c. buckwheat flour and 1 c. whole
wheat pastry flour to recipes.

WHEAT AND SOY: 1 c. finely ground soy flour
or powder and 1 c. whole wheat pastry flour.

GREEN NOODLES: Cut down oil to 2 T., eggs to
2 (if used), and add 1/4 c. strained spinach,
kale, chard to either basic recipe.

ROLL OUT NOODLE DOUGH ON BREADBOARD DUSTED WITH ARROWROOT OR WHEAT FLOUR. CORN MEAL CAN ALSO BE USED FOR A LIGHT CORN TASTE.

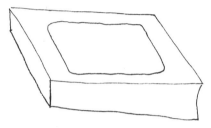

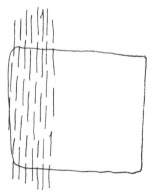

CUT DOUGH INTO THIN OR WIDE, LONG OR SHORT STRIPS.

SEMOLINA GNOCCI

This gnocci is like a little dumpling made from
tiny noodles. You can use cous-cous (fine) or
if you can't find that, use egg pastina made
preferably from semolina wheat.

4 c. milk
8 T. butter
3/4 parmesan cheese
1 c. semolina
1/2 t. salt

Scald milk, salt and 1 T. butter. When it
reaches scalding temperature, sprinkle in semolina, whisking with wire brush to keep smooth.
Cover and cook slowly 30 min. Stir in 1 T.
cheese. Dampen a board or tray and spread out
semolina mixture in a 1/2" thick rectangle.
Smooth top and let cool 30 min. Cut in 1 1/2"
squares (or smaller if you like.) Melt remaining butter and put 1/2 into a rectangular
bake pan. Arrange gnocci in pan, overlapping
slightly. Sprinkle with cheese and pour remaining butter on top. Bake 30 min. at 375°
until browned. This is so good alone, with
broth poured over it, or sauce, melted garlic-
butter, vegetables.

PINK-VIOLET FLOWERS

WILD MARJORAM

SOUP DUMPLINGS

This is one of the first things I learned to
cook from good old Mom. Boil 1 c. water and
1 c. butter (add 1/2 t. salt if unsalted butter
is used.) Add 1 c. of either whole wheat pastry flour, finely ground rice or barley flour
and beat smooth. Allow to cool a bit. Add 3
eggs, one at a time, and beat smooth. Drop in
boiling soup and cover. Cook 25 min. Don't
peek. Turn off fire and serve. Or drop in
boiling salted water and cook as above. Drain
and serve with sauce or vegetables, or add
vegetables, water and all, to soup and simmer
together 10 min.

SPAETZELS

2 c. whole wheat pastry flour
3 eggs
2/3 c. milk
1/2 c. bread crumbs
1/4 c. butter or oil
1 1/2 t. salt
1 T. dry parsley
basil, pepper, nutmeg

Mix together flour, milk, eggs, salt and a dash
or 2 each of basil, pepper and nutmeg in a
colander over a large kettle of boiling water.
Force flour mixture through colander with a
greased heavy object. Boil 5 min. stirring occasionally. Wash under cold water and drain.
Heat the oil and add bread crumbs. Stir until
brown over low heat. Stir in spaetzels and
brown, sprinkle with parsley. Can be eaten
plain or with butter, sauce, vegetables. Enough
little noodles for 4-6 people.

POTATO DUMPLING   (No. 1)

1 c. mashed potatoes (with skins, of course)
1 c. water
1/4 lb. butter
1/2 c. flour
3 eggs

Bring water and butter to boil. Beat in potato and flour. Then add eggs, one at a time,
and cook in any other dumpling way. You may
add to pot of sauerkraut and simmer covered in
the juice 25 min.

NO-EGG POTATO DUMPLING   (No. 2)

1 c. water
1 c. potato flour
1 c. soy butter
1/2 t. salt

Heat water to boil and add salt. Whip smooth
with flour. Then beat in soy butter and cook
as other dumplings.

MAKING SPAETZELS

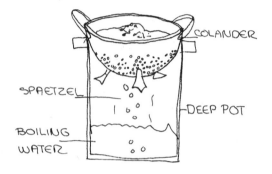

COLANDER

SPAETZEL

DEEP POT

BOILING
WATER

SPINACH DUMPLINGS   (With Eggs)

1 1/2 c. spinach, strained or pureed
1 c. finely ground flour
1/4 lb. butter or 1 c. soy butter
3 eggs (if butter is used)

Melt butter in sauce pan, add strained spinach
and bring to boil. Add flour and follow soup
dumpling recipe.

SPINACH DUMPLINGS   (Without Eggs)

Bring strained spinach to a boil and add 1/4 t.
salt and 1 c. flour. Cool slightly and whip
in, a little at a time, 1 c. soy butter. Cook
in a steamer over boiling water, as well as
any of the other ways.

ALL ABOUT BREAD STUFFINGS

Stuff squash, cabbage leaves, other stuffable
vegetables like cauliflower, onions, mushroom
caps, peppers...or bake stuffing separately in
a loaf pan as a side dish, or use as one of the
layers of a vegetable pie or casserole.

BREAD STUFFING - BASIC RECIPE

1/2 lb. bread (I like sprouted whole wheat)
1 med. onion, chopped fine
2 cloves garlic, chopped
1 c. hot water
1 t. salt or 2 T. tamari
3 T. oil

Break or cut bread in little pieces. Saute
garlic and onion in 1 T. oil first for 1-2 min.
or add raw to bread along with water, oil and
salt. Mix well and let sit together 30-60 min.
If you want herbs, add any of these along with
other ingredients:
1/2 t. basil

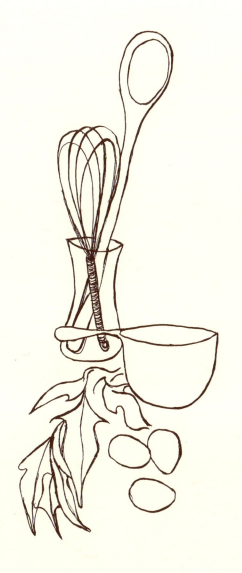

1 t. oregano
1/4 t. cayenne
1/2 t. ground coriander
2 T. dry parsley
1 T. paprika
2 T. sage
1 t. dry horseradish - 2 T. fresh, grated
1/2 t. fennel or caraway seeds
2 t. chervil

It's up to you to choose.
When mixture has set, stuff whatever you choose.
Winter squash should be boiled and pre-baked
20 min. at 375-400°, filled immediately and re-
turned to oven for 25 min. more of baking. It's
best to bake covered in an old roasting pan.
Cabbage, cabbage leaves, cauliflower, onion,
peppers should be steamed for 10-15 min., the
center cavity made and stuffed then with bread
mixture and baked at 375° for 20-25 min., un-
cover last 10 min. Usually, mushroom caps and
summer squash need no pre-cooking. Fill them
and bake 25-30 min. at 375°, of course; the
scooped out center of a vegetable should be
used in whatever stuffing recipe you choose.

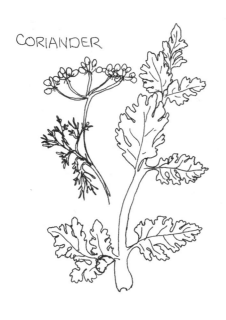

CORIANDER

CELERY BREAD STUFFING

To basic stuffing recipe add 2 t. celery seed
and 6 stalks finely chopped celery, green and
all. This is good with a little sweet pepper
in it, too.

MUSHROOM BREAD STUFFING

Add 1/2 lb. sliced mushrooms and a touch of
ground ginger or a few gratings of fresh, to
bread stuffing.

CORN BREAD STUFFING

Add 1 c. corn and 1/2 sweet red pepper finely
chopped. Use milk or milk substitute in place
of water.

CORNBREAD BREAD STUFFING

You need 4-6 leftover pieces of cornbread broken up for this one plus 1/4 c. maple syrup or honey, and 2-3 grated carrots. Mix with basics and use to stuff winter squash.
Use 1-2 grated sweet potatoes instead of or with carrots.

CHESTNUT BREAD STUFFING

To basic or celery stuffing recipe, add 1/2 c. cooked chestnuts, chopped in pieces or 1/2 c. roasted chestnuts. Mix and then you may stuff onions and cabbage, too.

CHEESE BREAD STUFFING

Grate 1 lb. of your favorite cheese or use 1 lb. curd or cottage cheese and mix with celery, mushroom or cornbread stuffing, or the basic recipe. Good for stuffing anything.

RAISIN-NUT BREAD STUFFING

To basic recipe add 1/2 c. raisins or currants (I like currants) and 1/4 lb. of chopped nuts, mixed or of the same type. Mix with 2 t. cinnamon and 1/4 t. allspice.   Substitute 1 c. of milk for water and stuff onions, winter squash, bake as a pudding...

12
MY FAVORITES

STUFFED CABBAGE ROLLS

2 c. cooked barley
1 med. onion
sweet corn scraped from the cob of one ear
2 carrots cut in little pieces
8 outer cabbage leaves steamed 5 min. over
   boiling water
1 round t. curry powder
2 T. tamari
2 T. oil

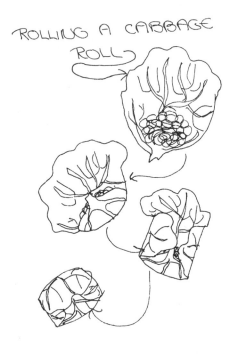

ROLLING A CABBAGE ROLL

Lightly roast curry powder in oil. Add onion
and stir, then carrot and last, corn while stir-
frying. When almost done, add barley and tamari
and mix well. Fill the cabbage by placing barley mixture at stalk end, rolling over once,
fold in sides and continue rolling to end of
the leaf. Place loose end down in lightly oiled
baking dish. Bake at 350° for 20 min. and
serve. (for 4)
Pour cream or tomato sauce over cabbage rolls
and bake until bubbly.

MAIFUN STUFFED ZUCCHINI

Maifun is a noodle-like food that is made from
rice or beans and is transparent when cooked.
It can be found in most oriental food stores
called maifun, py maifun, rice or bean threads.

1 very lg. zucchini or 3 med. sized
1 8 oz. package maifun
1 carrot
1 onion
1 stalk celery
2 T. tahini
1/4 c. roasted sunflower seeds
2 T. tamari
2 T. oil
1 T. fresh grated ginger

Soak maifun several hours or overnight, drain
and stir into boiling salted water until just
tender. Drain and rinse with cold water. Cut
lg. zucchini in half and scoop out all but 1/2"
thick shell. With small zucchini cut off stem

end and scoop out as much of inside as you can
with an apple corer or paring knife, leaving
enough to make a solid shell to be filled.
Chop remaining insides and other vegetables into thin, small pieces. Mix together with maifun, seeds, tahini, oil, tamari, and ginger.
Fill hollow zucchini and lay two halves or 3
smaller stuffed zucchini in lightly greased baking dish. Cover and put in 375° oven for 25
min. (serves 6)
For an extra treat, serve topped with mushroom
gravy.

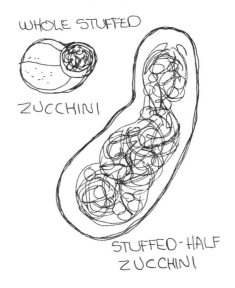

WHOLE STUFFED
ZUCCHINI

STUFFED-HALF
ZUCCHINI

KASHA-CORN STUFFED ACORN SQUASH

3 sm. acorn squash
2 c. cooked kasha
1 c. fresh raw corn
1 stalk broccoli
1/2 c. mung bean sprouts
2 sprigs parsley
1 clove garlic, crushed
2 T. tamari
2 T. oil

Halve and clean out acorn squash and bake open
side down on lightly oiled pan at 375° for 20
min. Chop vegetables, including garlic, in
thin little pieces and mix with all other ingredients. Turn squash with spatula and fill
center cavity of each. Bake covered in 375°
oven for 20 min. (serves 6)
Lay pieces of your favorite cheese over stuffed
squash for last 5 min. of baking and leave cover
off for that time.
I have found blue and white speckled, enamel
roasting pans to be perfect for foods that need
to be covered while baking, and they are only a
few dollars.

STUFFED ACORN
SQUASH HALVES

CHEESE AND NUT STUFFED ONIONS

Parboil 6 lg. onions in water for 20 min. Remove sm. part of center and fill with a mixture
of 1 c. celery, 1/2 c. chopped nuts, and 1/2 t.
salt. Bake in oiled pan sprinkled with 1/2 lb.
grated cheese for 20 min. at 350°.

NUT-STUFFED EGGPLANT

Cut 2 med. size eggplants in half and steam
for 10 min. in boiling water. Scoop out, putting the chopped up insides in a mixing bowl.
Chill the hollow eggplant. Saute in 2 T. oil
a few min.:

1 lg. onion
3 ripe tomatoes, chopped
1/2 green pepper
1 lb. coarse ground mixed nuts
1/2 c. water
2 T. tamari

Fill inside of eggplant with mixture of sauteed
veggies, nuts, and chopped squash insides. Put
in pan with a small bit of water and bake in
oven at 375° for 25 min.
Put some grated cheese on for the last 10 min.
of baking.

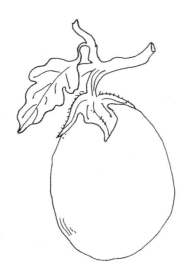

EGGPLANT

DARK PURPLE

STUFFED UPSIDE-DOWN CAULIFLOWER

Steam a lg. head of cauliflower for 10 min. in
boiling water. Remove core and hollow out a
hole to hold filling. Chill.

1 sweet red pepper
2 onions
3 chopped tomatoes
2 turnips with greens (if possible)
med. sized bunch of greens if you can't find
   turnips with greens
1 lg. butternut or buttercup squash
2 T. oil
2 T. tamari

First, saute the onions in heated oil. Add
squash, turnip and pepper, mix and cook covered 5 min. Add greens and tomatoes and mix in
tamari. Fill the cauliflower with the mixture
and spread the rest in oiled pan around cauliflower. Smooth oil on surface of cauliflower.
Bake at 375° for 20 min. Remove and eat.
 (serves 4)

Try pouring a mixture of juice from 2 lemons, 1/4 c. water and 1/3 c. oil over cauliflower during the last 10 min. of baking.

STUFFED PEPPERS

Cut off tops of 6 lg. peppers and clean out the inside. Steam in water 5 min. and cool. Fill with one of the following things or your own favorite and bake in 375° oven for 20 min.

Tomato-rice filling:
2 c. cooked rice
1 med. onion, chopped
4 lg. tomatoes, chopped
chopped up tops of the green peppers
1 t. oregano
1 T. oil
2 T. tamari

Mix together.

Cheese and nut filling:
1 lb. crumbled feta or cottage cheese
1 t. salt
1 T. oil
1/2 lb. chopped nuts
1 bunch scallions
1 t. basil

Mix together.

Kasha-cottage cheese filling:
2 c. cooked kasha
1 lb. cottage cheese
2 t. caraway seeds
1 T. paprika
1 t. salt
1 T. oil

Mix together.

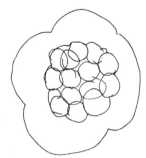

STUFFED PEPPER

GARLIC

SWEET CORN

RICE AND VEGETABLE GUMBO

4 c. cooked rice
1/4 lb. green beans
1 lg. onion
1 green pepper
1 c. fresh corn
3 ripe tomatoes
2 okra
1 t. celery seed
1/2 t. tarragon
2 T. oil
1 t. salt

Saute vegetables together in oil for 2-3 min.
Mix in rice, salt and herbs and bake in oiled
dish at 350° for 25 min.   (serves 6-8)

MEATLESS BALLS AND GRAVY

2 c. cooked kasha (cooked mushy)
2 sprigs chopped parsley
1 bunch scallions or 1 lg. onion
1/4 c. roasted sesame seeds
1/2 c. whole or buckwheat flour
1 carrot, grated
2 T. oil
3 T. tamari
1/2 t. oregano
1/2 t. ground or crushed coriander
1/4 t. basil

Mix 1 T. tamari and all other ingredients,
chopping vegetables in tiny pieces. Form into
little balls, dipping hands in cold water to
prevent sticking. Coat balls with some flour
and brown well on all sides in lightly oiled
skillet. Cover and simmer over low flame for
10 min. Remove from pan into serving dish.
For gravy: Immediately add 2 T. more of oil to
scrapings in skillet and mix in 2 T. buckwheat
flour to make a paste. Slowly add 2 c. water,
whisking with wire whip to prevent lumps.
Stir until hot and thick, add remaining 2 T.
tamari. Pour over meatless balls and serve
alone or over noodles or mashed potatoes.
(6-8 servings)

MUSHROOM-CHEESE BAKE

1 lb. mushrooms (wash and leave whole)
1 lb. carrots
1 lb. onions
1 lb. melty cheese (swiss is great)
2 T. oil
2 T. tamari

Bake chopped vegetables, oil, mushrooms, and
cheese together in dish at 400° for 20 min.
Add tamari and bake 5 more min. Eat.
(serves 4)

BAKED KASHA AND MUSHROOMS

Add 4 c. cooked kasha to above recipe and bake
as directed. (serves 6-8)

SOUR CREAM BAKED MUSHROOMS

2 lb. little mushrooms
2 c. sour cream
1 bunch scallions
2 cloves garlic, crushed
1 T. tamari or 1 t. salt
paprika

Mix together and bake sprinkled with paprika
in lightly oiled pan at 375° for 25 min. Serve
it on little pieces of toast, muffins, noodles.
(serves 6)
Substitute yoghurt for sour cream.

WILD
ONION

GREEN CHEESE LOAF

2 lb. melty cheese
1 bunch chopped fresh parsley
1 bunch chopped scallions

Slice cheese and layer it with scallions, cheese
again and parsley. Continue this, ending with
cheese. Bake 30 min. at 350°. Slice and eat
plain, on a sandwich, with vegetables on top,
any way you like.

BAKED SPAGHETTI

1 8 oz. pkg. buckwheat spaghetti
1 lg. onion, chopped
1 c. cooked kidney or lentil beans
1 c. cooked kasha
3/4 c. grated cheese
1/2 lb. sliced mushrooms
2 c. stewed tomatoes
1/4 c. oil
1/2 t. salt

Saute onions and garlic a bit till onion begins
to soften. Add mushrooms and tomatoes. Put
1/2 the spaghetti in a greased baking dish.
Then add 1 c. kasha and beans, salt and pepper
sprinkled on with tomato sauce on top. Bake
at 375° for 25 min. Add the cheese for 5 more
min. and serve. (for 6)

BIRD HANGING
FROM SKY BAND

LIMA BEAN LOAF

2 c. cooked limas (fresh), dry limas are an
  okay substitute
1 c. bread or cracker crumbs
1 sm. chopped onion
1/2 c. chopped nuts
1/2 c. cream or sesame milk
1/4 c. soy flour, roasted
parsley
1/2 t. salt
2 T. oil

Mix it all up, press it into a greased loaf
pan and bake 45 min. at 350°. Baste the top
with oil once in awhile. Sprinkle parsley on
top when baked.

WHEAT

VEGETABLE-CORN BALLS

2 c. cornmeal
1 med. onion
1 carrot
1 turnip
1 c. whole wheat flour
2 T. tamari
oil for deep frying
water

Chop vegetables fine and mix all ingredients
with just enough water to make a batter thick
enough to form into walnut size balls. Roll
in a little cornmeal and fry 3 or 4 at a time
in deep oil heated to 350°. Remove when golden brown and drain well. Serve alone or with
sesame sauce. (enough for 6-8 portions)

LENTIL CROQUETTES WITH MUSHROOM GRAVY

3 c. cooked lentils
1 lg. onion, finely chopped
2 c. cornmeal
1/2 c. whole wheat flour
1 carrot, chopped fine
2 T. oil
2 T. tamari

Mix everything together and if too dry, add a
little water. Shape into little eggs and fry
in deep oil until well browned on all sides.
Drain well and serve with buckwheat mushroom
gravy. (6 people, 3 each)

FRIED NOODLE CROQUETTES

4 c. cooked macaroni or broken noodles
2 T. chopped dry parsley or 3 stalks chopped
1 c. grated cheese
1 sm. onion chopped
1 c. thick white sauce

Mix everything together and cool on a plate or
dish. Shape into little eggs and roll in flour
or cornmeal. Deep fry in 365-380° oil for 5
min.

RUTABAGA

PURPLE TOP
ORANGE BOTTOM

VEGETABLE CREAM SAUCE

1 sm. zucchini
1 clove garlic, crushed
1 med. onion
3 c. water
1/2 c. tahini
1 T. oil
2 T. tamari

Saute garlic and onion in oil for 2-3 min. Add
zucchini and cook covered for 5. min. Add 1 c.
of the water and tahini. Mix until smooth and
slowly add remaining water. Heat until somewhat thickened and add tamari. Pour on the
croquettes. (4 people get 3 each)

ONION PIE

4 big onions, any way you like them
3 sprigs parsley
1 green or red pepper (if you like)
1 T. paprika
2 c. water
3 T. oil
1/2 c. flour
3 T. tamari
double pie crust recipe (enough for top and
    bottom)

Dust onion with paprika-flour mixture and put
it all in the heated oil. Stir and saute until flour and onion are mixed with oil. Add
pepper and parsley. Stir and slowly add boiling water or stock. Mix smooth with tamari
and pour into crust-lined pie pan. Cover with
top-crust, poke a few holes to let out air and
baste the crust with a bit of oil. Bake at
400° for 25 min. (serves 6)

ONION-CHEESE PIE

Make an onion pie. Before putting the top
crust on, lay 1 lb. sliced swiss, cheddar,
muenster, colby or mixture on onions. A sprinkle of caraway is good here. Bake the same
way.

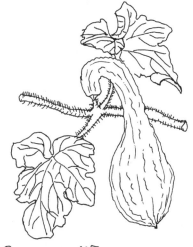

YELLOW
CROOK-NECK
SUMMER SQUASH

MUSHROOM STROGANOFF

1 lb. mushrooms (little)
2 bunches of scallions or 3 med. red onions
4 c. tomato sauce or 1 1/2 c. tomato paste and
  3 c. water
3 cloves garlic, crushed
1 pt. (16 oz.) yoghurt or soured cream
2 T. olive oil, if possible
2 t. caraway seeds
1/2 t. oregano
1 t. basil
3 T. tamari

Heat oil and add caraway seeds, garlic, and
onions. Saute until onions get golden. Add
mushrooms, stir a min. and add tomato paste
and herbs. Cook covered for 15 min. Turn
off and add tamari. Serve on rice or noodles
along with yoghurt to spoon on or cool a bit
and stir in yoghurt before serving.
(enough for 4 people)

CREAMY BAKED MACARONI

1 lb. whole grain macaroni (cook according to
  package directions or your own)
3 c. white sauce or tahini sauce
paprika
oil

Mix drained noodles with the sauce and 1/2 t.
salt. Spread in oiled bake dish. Dust with
paprika and bake 20 min. Cool a bit and eat.

MACARONI AND CHEESE

Saute 1 lb. macaroni or broken flat noodles
along with 3 cloves crushed garlic until browned. Add either 4 c. of half cream and half
milk (or add 1 c. tahini mixed with 3 c. water), 1 lb. melting cheese and 1 t. salt.
Sprinkle with paprika and bake at 400° for 20
min. until noodles absorb liquid.

LOOK IN RICH, DAMP SOIL IN OR NEAR WOODS.

GREEN AND FETA CHEESE PIE

1/2 lb. of your favorite greens (mustard greens are fantastic)
1 lb. feta cheese, crumbled
1 lg. onion, diced
3 or 4 sprigs parsley, chopped
tamari
1 carrot, grated
1 T. oil
1/2 c. water
1 pie crust

Chop greens well and mix with cheese, onion, parsley, and tamari to taste. Fill pie shell very full with mixture and sprinkle top with grated carrot. Mix oil with water and sprinkle over top of pie. Bake 20-25 min. in 350° oven.

BAKED KASHA AND NOODLES

Take 4 c. cooked kasha, 1 lb. cooked noodles and 2 lg. onions and saute in oil till tender. Mix together with 1 T. paprika, 2 T. poppy seeds, 2 T. tamari, and 1 qt. yoghurt. Bake it in an oiled square or rectangle at 400° for 20 min. Cool a bit and eat. (serves 8)

BAKED KASHA AND NOODLES WITH CHEESE

Add 1 lb. of melting cheese or feta to the mixture and bake it the same way as above. You'll get a good cheesey treat.

BAKED CARAWAY NOODLES IN YOGHURT

2 lb. flat noodles
2 T. caraway seeds
2 T. tamari
1 qt. yoghurt
2 T. oil
1 t. basil

Cook noodles in salt water, drain and rinse. Heat oil and roast caraway seeds for a min. Add noodles, basil, and tamari and stir well. Add yoghurt and bake at 400° for 20 min.

PARSNIP

WILD PARSNIPS LOOK AND TASTE LIKE THE GARDEN KIND AND CAN BE PICKED FOR COOKING GREEN TOPS IN EARLY SPRING AND FOR THE ROOT FROM SPRING UNTIL PLANT FLOWERS, AND ROOT BECOMES TOUGH AND FIBROUS.

SAUERKRAUT AND DUMPLINGS

1 lg. onion
2 carrots, sliced
6 c. sauerkraut
1 batch of egg dumplings or soy wheat dumplings
2 T. oil
1 T. caraway seed
1 t. salt

Saute onion and caraway in oil a min. Add carrot, stir and saute covered until carrot is almost tender. Mix in sauerkraut and tamari. Lay dumplings cooked in salt water or stock on top of kraut. Cover and steam together 10 min. (enough for 8)

VEGETANANDA-SOBA SOUP

2 c. cornmeal
1 c. whole wheat pastry flour
2 1/2 c. water
1 t. salt
1 carrot
1/2 sm. winter squash with seeds
1 bunch chopped scallions
2 sprigs parsley

Chop vegetables in tiny, tiny pieces and mix with other ingredients. Chill well. Heat oil to 350° and drop batter by wooden spoonfuls into oil, frying until golden brown. (If the vegetable cakes do not pop to the surface of the oil immediately, the oil is not hot enough). Remove from oil and drain well.

SOBA SOUP

1 lb. pkg. soba (buckwheat noodles)
2 qts. water
1/4 c. miso
1 T. fresh grated ginger
3 T. tamari
1 T. oil

Bring water to boil and add noodles, oil, and ginger. Cook until noodles are done, about 7-10 min. Remove from heat and add miso, soft-

MUSHROOMS

IT IS BEST TO PICK JUST A FEW WELL-KNOWN EDIBLES WHEN BEGINNING TO GATHER, AND THE BEST WAY TO LEARN IS FROM A VETERAN MUSHROOM GATHERER.

COLLYBIA

VELVET-STEMMED COLLYBIA

MASS ON TREE TRUNKS. YELLOW TO VELVETY BROWN WITH AGE.

ened in a bit of water and tamari. Put in 4 big soup bowls or 6 med. size and lay vegeta-nanda cakes on top. (serves 4-6)

CORN-MUSHROOM LOAF

3 c. cooked kasha
1/2 lb. mushrooms, chopped
1 qt. yoghurt
corn from 6 ears or 2 c. corn
3 stalks fresh parsley chopped or 2 T. dry
2 T. tamari
2 T. oil
paprika

Mix all the ingredients together. Sprinkle with paprika and bake in lg. loaf pan or a square baking dish at 375° for 25 min. (for 6)

CORN-MUSHROOM LOAF WITH NOODLES

Cook 1/2 lb. noodles in salt water, drain and mix with other ingredients. Bake the same way. (for 8)

TAMARI-GARLIC NOODLES

1 lb. any kind of whole grain noodles
3 cloves garlic, crushed and chopped
2 T. oil
2 T. tamari

Cook noodles in boiling water until just ten-der. Drain and rinse with cold water. Heat oil and saute garlic 2 or 3 min. until lightly browned. Add noodles and tamari and stir un-til hot. (serves 6)

TAHINI NOODLES

Follow directions for garlic noodles adding 3 T. tahini with the tamari.

SUNFLOWER NOODLES

Follow recipe for garlic noodles, omitting garlic and roasting 1/2 c. sunflower seeds in dry pan before adding oil, noodles, and tamari. Sesame seeds may be substituted for sunflower seeds.
1 c. of mung bean or alfalfa sprouts can be added with the noodles. Add a chopped onion or 1 bunch chopped scallions. Saute until golden in the oil before adding noodles.

CRANBERRY BORSCHT

Cook 1 lb. raw cranberries with a little water covered on med. heat for 25 min. While they cook chop:

1 lg. onion
1 sm. red cabbage
1 bunch beets (3-4) with tops if possible
3 cloves garlic, crushed
1 T. caraway
2 T. paprika
1 t. basil
oil

Saute the caraway, paprika, onion, garlic, beets, and beet tops in oil for a few min. Add cabbage after the other ingredients have cooked for awhile. Add cranberries with the juice, basil and 1/4 c. arrowroot dissolved in 1/3 c. water. Stir until hot and thick. Stir in 3 T. tamari or 1 1/2 t. salt and serve on noodles or rice. (makes 8 servings)
Sour cream or yoghurt can be served on top.

THE LITTLE GREY COLLYBIA IS EASY TO FIND. THE GILLS ARE BROAD AND FLAT AND MERGE WITH THE STEM RATHER THAN THE STEM BEING SET INTO THE GILLS. THE TOP OF THE CAP IS SMOKEY GREY, THE UNDERSIDE IS CREAMY WHITE.

CABBAGE-BEET BORSCHT

Make this as you would the cranberry borscht but leave out the cranberries and arrowroot and increase the cabbage to 1 lg. head. The rest is the same.

WHITE
POTATO

SPROUT SANDWICHES

The health food store on the village green in
Woodstock serves these and I got the basic idea
from them. First make a good thick dressing.
I like vegetable water, tahini, garlic, dill
(and/or other herbs), lemon juice or umeboshi
plums and tamari soy sauce mixed together. If
you have a blender or grain grinder, sunflower
seeds make a great thick creamy dressing in
place of tahini. Pumpkin seeds, too. Spread
it on two slices of sprouted bread if you can
get it or make it, or good whole grain bread.
Put a big pile of sprouts on (alfalfa is the
best, I think, and maybe a few fenugreek
sprouts with it). Close it together and eat
cold, toast a bit in oven or grill in a little
oil on top of stove. If you like cheese, put
some on, onion slices, garlic, lots of things.
My favorite is sprouts, cheese and a toasted
sheet of nori seaweed. (Hold it over flame,
not too close, until color turns green and
bright. It burns easily, so wave it around
and it won't catch fire). Toast till the
cheese melts. Pickles are good, too.

LARRY'S PATTIE MELTS

In a little oil, saute 1 lg. sliced onion until
golden brown and transparent. Put spread or
butter on four slices of bread. Divide onion
up on the slices and top with your favorite
melting cheese, a layer of grated carrot, a
few slices of cucumber and another slice of
bread with spread. Grill in covered skillet
till brown or toast in oven.

LATKES SANDWICH

Make 4 big potato latkes like the recipe in
the vegetable section. Put spread on four
slices of bread. Add slices of your favorite
cheese. Put sprouts and a potato pancake on
each and cover with a slice of bread with
spread. Bake on griddle or in oven until
cheese begins to melt. (4 big sandwiches)

5 ROCK CITY SANDWICH

8 1/2" thick slices unyeasted bread
3 sprigs parsley, chopped fine
grated goat's cheese
onion, lightly sauteed
miso-tahini spread
alfalfa sprouts

Spread bread with miso-tahini. Add sauteed
onion, alfalfa sprouts and cheese. Sprinkle
top with parsley. Place in hot oven for 7-10
min. until cheese is melted and serve.

FALAFEL

4 c. ground chick peas or chick pea flour
2 T. curry powder
1 T. paprika
1/2 t. coriander
1 t. cumin seeds
2 T. caraway seeds
1 t. crushed red hot pepper
1/2 t. each of basil, oregano, thyme
1/4 c. oil
2 T. tamari
1 lg. onion
2 T. parsley
boiling water

CAYENNE PEPPER

Mix all ingredients together and add enough
boiling water to make a thick batter that can
be formed into ping-pong size balls that hold
their form solidly. Put the balls on a plate
and let sit in refrigerator until cold. It's
not necessary to chill them, but I find they
cook crisper that way. Drop 3-4 balls at a
time in deep oil, 350°, until well browned all
around. Drain well and serve. They are used
in a sandwich made of "pita", a round, flat,
syrian yeast bread with a hollow pocket in the
center. A sm. slice is taken off one side and
the pocket is stuffed with 1 or 2 falafel, raw
onion, tomato, lettuce and cucumber slices.
Then a sauce is poured inside to finish it off.
(A slice of feta is good, too).

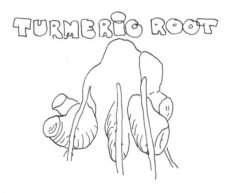

TURMERIC ROOT

(See next page for falafel sauce.)

WHEN GATHERING WILD MUSHROOMS, TAKE A KNIFE TO SLICE OFF AT BASE OF STEM SO THE UNDERGROUND PORTION CAN BE LEFT TO REGENERATE ..

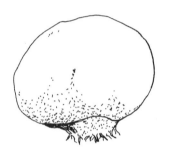

PUFFBALL

PICK WHEN YOUNG AND WHITE. INSIDE IS AN OFF YELLOW COLOR. A LIGHT LITTLE MUSHROOM TO SEE PERCHED ON ROTTING WOOD IN FORESTS OR GRASSY FIELDS.

Falafel Sauce: (cont'd. from preceding page)

1/2 c. tahini
2 c. water
juice of 2 lemons
2 T. tamari
1/4 c. oil
1 t. ground or crushed cumin seed
1 clove garlic, crushed and chopped

Beat water slowly into tahini and then add remaining ingredients.
Falafel is also used alone like a meatball with the tahini sauce over it. I sometimes heat the sauce before using it.
Fava beans may be used in place of chick peas and, in fact, I prefer their lightness although they are less common.

SCALLOPED CORN

corn from 12 ears or 6 c. corn
1 onion
3 c. milk or 3/4 c. tahini mixed with 2 1/2 c. water
4 T. flour
1 t. salt

Mix corn, salt, onion, and flour and spread in a greased baking dish. Pour milk over it and bake at 375° for 30 min. (enough for 6)

NORI-ADUKI RICE ROLLS

4 c. cooked rice
3 c. cooked aduki beans
1/2 c. roasted sesame seeds
2 T. oil
3 T. tamari
10 sheets nori (laver)

Mix all ingredients and roll in nori, tucking in one end to make eating easier. Bake at 400° on greased cookie sheet for 25 min. Eat hot or cold.

ADUKI PIZZA

4 c. aduki beans (cover them with water and
   soak several hours, preferably overnight)
2 good-sized onions, chopped
1/2 green pepper, minced
several cloves garlic, minced
favorite cheese, about 1/2 lb.
1/2 c. oil
1 T. oregano
1 t. marjoram
2 t. salt
1 t. basil
tamari to taste
pizza dough*

*Pizza dough: Soften 1/2 t. dry yeast in 1 c.
warm water and add 1 t. salt and 2 T. oil. Mix
in 3-4 c. whole wheat flour until soft and elastic. Knead a short while and set in warm place,
covered, to rise (about 1 hour.) When risen,
punch down, let it rest 10-20 min. and press
onto greased cookie sheet or pizza pan or lg.
iron skillet.
If you're not into pizza, use the same dough
and filling, only roll or press balls of dough
into circles and fill with the bean stuff and
cheese, fold over, press edges with fork, put
on greased cookie sheet, brush with oil and
bake 20-35 min. at 350°.

Drain aduki beans, saving juice. While they
drain, chop vegetables and grate cheese. Grind
beans through a meat grinder (it's really worth
it to get a meat grinder to make your own meat
substitutes because the canned stuff is usually
garbage). Put 1 t. of the oil into pan and
saute garlic, onion, and green pepper slightly.
Add ground aduki beans and remaining oil and
also herbs, salt, and tamari to taste. Stir
together a few min. over med.-high flame. Add
about 2 c. of water from soaked adukis, stir,
turn down flame, and cover, letting it cook until water is absorbed. If beans still seem a
little hard, add another c. of water and cook
a little longer. They should have a rough
texture, not be mushy. Spread this mixture onto cookie sheet lined with pizza dough. Top
with grated cheese and bake at 375° for 20 min.

ROUGH STEMMED BOLETUS

THE BOLETUS FAMILY IS ABUNDANT WITH EDIBLES. ALL ARE RECOGNIZABLE BY THE SPONGE UNDERSIDE OF THE CAP.

CAP WHITE, BROWN OR SMOKEY OR RED -- TURNS DARK WHEN BRUISED

FOUND IN WOODS OR GRASSY PLACES

THIS SHELF MUSHROOM
IS BRIGHT RED AND
MAY HAVE A YELLOW
UNDERSIDE. ALSO
CALLED "CHICKEN
MUSHROOM"
BECAUSE OF A
TEXTURE AND TASTE
SIMILARITY.

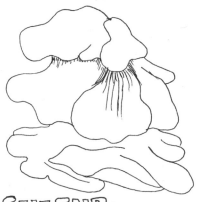

SULFUR-
COLORED
POLY PORE

LIVES ON DEAD OR
ALIVE WOODY
PLANTS.

SPRING ROLLS

2 stalks celery
1 c. sprouts, mung bean or alfalfa
2 carrots
1 bunch scallions
2 sprigs parsley
1 stalk broccoli
1/2 t. fresh grated ginger
2 T. tamari
1 T. oil
2 crust pie dough with sesame seeds

Chop vegetables very small and thin and mix
with other ingredients. Divide pie dough into 6 equal parts. Roll one out into a square
about 1/8" thick. Spoon on some of vegetable
mixture. Roll up, folding in the ends. Do
the same with all six and drop into 360° deep
oil, 2 at a time, cooking until golden brown.
Drain well and eat hot or cold.

VEGETABLE-CHICK PEA TURNOVERS

4 c. cooked chick peas
1 chopped green pepper
3 chopped stalks celery
2 T. oil
2 cut carrots
1 cut onion, lg.
2 T. paprika
3 T. tamari

Add onion and paprika to heated oil. Stir and
saute for 2 min. Mix in carrot and cover for
5 min. Add the pepper and celery and stir.
Mix in chick peas and tamari. Fill squares of
pie dough and fold into triangles sealing edges.
Poke a few holes in each and bake on lightly
greased cookie sheet in 400° oven for 30 min.,
until brown.

MOREL
(SPONGE MUSHROOM)
FOUND IN MOST OF
THE UNITED STATES.
DELICIOUS. GOLD-
BROWN CAP WITH
LIGHTER VEINS AND
STEM.

CANTHEREL
AN EDIBLE LITTLE
FUNNEL SMOKEY
COLORED TO BROWN.
YOUNG MUSHROOM
IS COVERED WITH
FOLDS ON THE
UNDERSIDE.

13
PICKLES, JAMS
& JELLIES

CROCK CUCUMBER DILLS

Use a 5 gal. crock. In the bottom, put a layer of dill and sprinkle in a little mustard and garlic. Lay in a thick layer of washed cucumbers, another layer of dill and spice, more cucumbers, until crock is almost full. Cover cucumbers with a brine of 1 lb. salt to 10 qts. water and 1 qt. apple cider vinegar. Cover with a layer of grape leaves if you can find some and cheese cloth, big enough to overlap sides of crock. Invert a plate and set a gal. jug filled with water on top as a weight. Let stand 2-3 weeks. Pack pickles in hot sterile jars, bring brine from crock to a boil, pour over pickles and seal jars. Process 15 min. in boiling water.
Crock pickling may be done with plastic instead of cheese cloth. For a stronger, sourer pickle, use 2-3 qts. more vinegar and cut back 2-3 qts. of water.

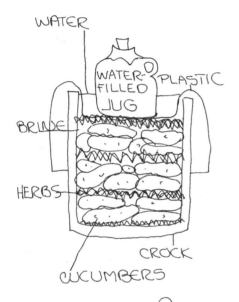

WATER
WATER-FILLED JUG
PLASTIC
BRINE
HERBS
CROCK
CUCUMBERS

CROCK DILLS

WATERMELON RIND PICKLES

Rind from 1 lg. watermelon, remove outer skin and pink part of melon. Cut in pieces and cover with salt water, 1 qt. water to 1/2 c. salt. Let sit several hours or overnight. Drain and wash with cold water. Bring to a boil 1 qt. cider vinegar and 1 qt. water. Tie in a cheese cloth bag and boil in vinegar and water for 20 min. 2 cinnamon sticks, 1/2 t. allspice, 2 t. cloves, 1/2 t. coriander, and a few slices fresh ginger. After 20 min. add 1 c. honey and return to boil. Pack watermelon rind into hot, sterile pint jars (6) and cover with vinegar mixture. Seal. Store at least 2 wks.
If you like very sweet pickles, 1 1/2 - 2 c. honey can be used. Lemon slices add nice flavor.

QUICK PICKLES

2 c. carrots, cut in strips
1 chopped green pepper
1 chopped red pepper
3 chopped onions
1 c. of green beans in 1" pieces
1/2 t. paprika
1 1/2 t. salt
1/4 t. turmeric
1 c. vinegar

Combine vinegar and seasoning and cook until
mixture is boiling and thick. Add vegetables,
cook 5 min. and fill sterile, hot pts. Seal.
(makes 4 pints)

OIL AND CUCUMBER PICKLES

Slice 20 unpeeled cucumbers very thin. Cover
with a brine of 1/4 c. salt and 1 qt. water.
Set for 2-3 hours. Drain and rinse with cold
water. Pack in clean pint jars (2). Add 1/2 t.
mustard seed and 1 sm. onion, sliced, to each.
Put 1 t. celery seed in 1 1/2 c. cider vinegar
and simmer 20 min. Then add enough water to
make 1 1/2 c. again and slowly stir in 1/2 c.
olive oil. Pour over cucumber slices and seal.
Process 10 min.

CORN RELISH

8 c. corn, fresh from cob is best
1 t. celery seed
2 pts. vinegar (cider)
1/4 c. salt
1 sweet red pepper, chopped
1 lg. onion, chopped
2 pts. water

While vinegar, water, salt and celery seed boil
(for 15 min.), mix corn, onion, pepper together
and pack in hot sterile jars (10 - 1/2 pts.)
Pour boiling liquid over vegetables and seal.
Store at least 3 weeks.

BRUSSELS
SPROUTS

MEMBER OF TH CABBAGE
FAMILY. THE VEGETABLE
LOOKS LIKE LITTLE
CABBAGES.

APPLE-PEPPER RELISH

2 sweet peppers (1 red and 1 green)
2 lg. sweet onions
2/3 c. honey
3 apples, cored
1 T. grated lemon rind
1/3 c. fresh lemon juice
1 t. salt

Chop peppers, onions and apples or put through a food grinder. Add lemon rind and juice and bring to a boil. Add honey and salt and boil until thick. Stir once in a while. Put in 1/2 pt. jars (4) and seal.

CATSUP

4 c. pureed tomatoes
1 lg. chopped onion
2 cloves garlic
2 T. oil
1/2 c. cider vinegar
2/3 c. honey
2 T. salt
1 green pepper, chop
2 stalks celery, chopped
1/2 t. each cayenne, paprika, oregano, basil
1/2 c. raisins, pureed

Chop all vegetables fine or put through food grinder. Saute onion, celery, pepper, garlic and spice in oil for a few min. Add tomato-raisin puree and cook together with salt, vinegar and honey until thick. Stir occcassionally. Pack in sterile pint jars.(makes 3-4) Raisin puree is not a necessity if it's a problem to make.

WATERMELON RIND CHUTNEY

Grind up peeled white rind of 1 lg. watermelon. For every 3 lbs. rind (about 2 c.) add 3 c. honey, 1 c. lemon juice or cider vinegar, 1 c. water, 2 T. salt, 1 lg. chopped onion, and 1/2 lb. currants. Simmer 25 min., pack in 1/2 pt. (8) jars and seal.

CLOVES:
FROM A LARGE TREE

WATERMELON PRESERVES

4 qts. diced small watermelon, pink and white
  (remove peel of course)
4 c. honey
1/4 t. salt
slices of 1 lemon
2 sticks kanten
1/2 c. cider vinegar
2" stick cinnamon
1 t. cloves

Put watermelon in colander and squeeze out
juice. Soak agar-agar in juice for 20 min.
Simmer watermelon, spices, vinegar, lemon slices and salt for 30 min. Add kanten and juice,
simmer 15 min. more, stir in honey and seal in
1/2 pts. (4-6)

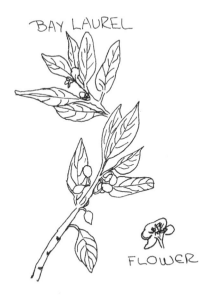

BAY LAUREL

FLOWER

MIXED FRUIT CHUTNEY

1 c. cider vinegar
1 1/2 c. honey
1 sm. cinnamon stick
1/2 t. coriander seed
2 T. salt
1/8 t. cayenne pepper
1 c. dry apricots
1 peeled canteloupe
1 c. water
dash of nutmeg
2 cardamom pods
2 cloves garlic, crushed and chopped
1 c. raisins
1 T. grated ginger

Tie spices in cheese cloth bag and add to vinegar and water along with cayenne and salt. Boil
15 min. and add ginger and dry fruit. Let sit
20 min. Peel and cut canteloupe in small chunks
and add to kettle. Bring to a boil, remove
spice bag and jar in 1/2 pt. jars (5). Process
10 min.

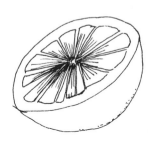

GRAPEFRUIT
HALF

FRUIT JUICE JELLY

1 qt. of apple, grape, apricot, currant or other
   fruit juice
juice of 4 lemons
2 bars agar-agar (kanten)
1 c. honey

Soak agar-agar in fruit juice 15 min. Bring
to gentle boil until agar-agar is dissolved.
Add honey and lemon, mix well and put in 1/2
pt. jars (5) and seal.

APPLE JELLY

3 lbs. apples
2 cinnamon sticks
8 c. water
4 c. honey
2 agar-agar sticks

Chop whole apples. Soak agar-agar in water
and boil with honey, cinnamon, and apples for
20 min. Remove to cheese cloth bag and allow
jelly to drip into pan. Heat to boil and jar
in 1/2 pts.   (makes a dozen)

GRAPE JELLY

5 lbs. grapes, either red, white or mixed
4 sticks agar-agar
juice of 4 lemons
2 c. water
5 c. honey

Soak agar-agar in water for 20 min. Boil gently with grapes for 30 min. in covered pan.
Strain into another pan and heat to a boil.
Mix in honey and lemon and jar.
(makes a dozen 1/2 pts)

CRANBERRY JELLY

Follow the recipe for grape jelly, substituting
3 lbs. cranberries for grapes and increasing
honey to 6 c. Use juice of 2 oranges instead
of lemon.

IRISH MOSS

USED FOR MAKING
GLOSS SOAP, PUDDING,
JELLY, FOR
CURING LEATHER
AND GLAZING
CLOTH.

HONEY-SPICE PEACH JAM

4 lbs. peaches
4 bars agar-agar
juice of 3 lemons
1/4 t. ground ginger
6 c. water
4 c. honey
1/2 t. ground allspice
1 t. ground cinnamon

Soak agar-agar in water for 20 min. Chop peaches into little pieces and boil with the water and spices 25 min. Add honey and lemon and mix well. Seal in 1/2 pt. jars (makes about 16)

PLUM JAM

Make plum jam by pitting 5 lbs. plums and following the directions for peach jam without the spices. (makes 14 to 16, 1/2 pt.)

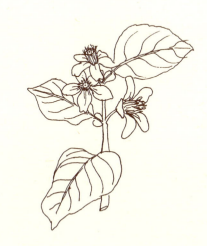

PEACH-PLUM JAM

Made by mixing 2 lbs. each of pitted peaches and plums and following the peach jam recipe with or without spices.

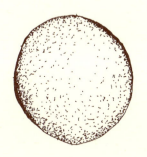

STRAWBERRY JAM

4 pts. fresh strawberries
4 sticks agar-agar
4 c. honey
4 c. water
rind and juice of 2 lemons

Soak agar-agar in water 15 min. Clean strawberries. Boil water and berries together for 25 min. Add honey and lemon and seal in 1/2 pt. (16).

14
PIES, COOKIES, CAKES
& GOODIES

APPLE KRUNCH

Cut up 6-7 apples into bite-sized slices; this makes a med. size apple krunch (9x12). Spread them on oiled dish. Add raisins or currants if you want. Mix together 3 parts rolled oats to 1 part flour (rice, whole wheat, rye, corn, whatever). Enough oil to lightly moisten, a dash of salt, some cinnamon to taste if you like it, sunflower seeds if you have some. Cover apples with crumbly stuff and lightly pat it down. Take 1 1/2 c. of apple juice or water and slowly pour it all over the top of the crust. Let it sit 20-30 min. and bake in 400° oven 20-25 min. until crust browns.

CRANBERRY-APPLE KRUNCH

1 lb. cranberries
2 lb. apples
1 1/2 c. honey
4 c. oats
1 c. flour (whole wheat pastry, rice, etc.)
1/2 t. salt
1 c. shredded coconut
1/2 c. oil
1/2 c. water

Cook cranberries and water until tender and add 1 c. of honey. Allow to sit while slicing apples thin and mixing flour, oats, cinnamon, coconut, 1/2 c. honey, salt and oil together. Mix cranberries with apple slices (save juice). Line oiled pan with fruit and pour on 1/2 the juice. Spread oat mixture on top and pour remaining juice over it. Bake as you would with the apple krunch.

CARROT-RAISIN CAKE

1 lb. carrots, grated
1/2 lb. raisins soaked in 1 c. water
1/2 lb. nuts, chopped
1/4 c. oil, butter or 1 c. soy butter
2 c. finely ground, light flour
1 t. vanilla extract
6 eggs, separated
3/4 c. honey
1/4 t. salt
1 t. baking soda (optional)
2 t. cinnamon

Steam grated carrots in a bit of water. Cream together oil, egg yolks, honey, vanilla and salt. Mix soda and cinnamon into flour. Add raisin and carrot to honey mixture, then add flour. Beat up for 2-3 min. Add nuts and fold in stiffly beaten egg whites. Fill greased bread pan 2/3 full and bake at 350° for 45-60 min.

YELLOW CAKE

3 c. fine, light flour (whole wheat pastry,
   rice, barley)
1 1/2 c. water
1 c. honey
1/2 c. oil, butter or 1 c. soy butter
6 eggs, separated
1 t. baking soda
1 c. chopped nuts
1/4 t. salt
1 t. vanilla

Cream butter, honey, vanilla, salt and egg yolks together. Add flour-soda mixture and water, a little at a time, and beat until smooth. Add nuts. Pour into greased square baking pan and bake at 350° for 30-35 min. Cool, cut and eat plain, with butter or frosted.

PIE CRUST

FOR FRUIT, BERRY AND VEGETABLE PIES:

FILL BOTTOM CRUST WITH YOUR CHOICE AND EITHER BAKE AT 400° FOR 30 MIN., OR TOP THE PIE WITH CRUST AND BAKE 10 MIN. AT 425° AND TURN DOWN TO 350° FOR 30 MIN. MORE.

BASTE TOP WITH SOY BUTTER OR BEATEN EGG FOR LAST 15 MIN. BAKING.

BANANA-LEMON-COOKIE CAKE

1 lb. vanilla wafers
6 bananas
recipe for lemon pie filling
1 c. heavy cream
2 T. honey

With 1/3 of the wafers, line bottom and some of sides of a lg. shallow glass or wooden bowl (a salad bowl works fine). Next add a layer of bananas. Then pour 1/3 of pie filling on. Do 3 layers like this and allow to set. Whip cream with honey and serve over cookie cake. Enough for 6-8 people.

CAROB BROWNIES   (Fudgey)

2 c. carob powder
1/2 c. arrowroot starch
1 c. finely ground, light flour
1 c. soy butter
1/4 t. salt
1/2 c. molasses
3/4 c. honey
1/2 c. sunflower seeds or chopped nuts
1 1/2-2 c. water
1 t. vanilla

Whip together soy butter, honey and molasses. Add carob, salt, arrowroot, flour and blend together. Add enough water to make thick, sticky batter. Add nuts. Spread out (3/4"-1" thick) on oiled bake pan and bake at 350° for 25-30 min.

CAROB-NUT CAKE

2 c. flour
1 c. carob powder
1 qt. yoghurt
1 c. water
1 c. nuts, chopped
1/2 c. oil, butter or 1 c. soy butter
6 eggs, separated
1 c. honey
1 t. baking soda

Blend ingredients as with the other cakes. Mix yoghurt with honey and oil before adding flour and water. Makes one small cake. Bake at 350° for 25-30 min.

...GIVE US THIS DAY OUR DAILY BREAD...

BASIC PIE CRUST (Double or 2 Single Crusts)

3 c. whole wheat pastry flour
1 c. soy butter or 3/4 c. oil
1/2 t. salt
boiling water (between 1 and 1 1/2 c., approx.)

With your fingers blend oil well with flour and salt. Mixture should be slightly damp. Add boiling water a bit at a time until dough is soft but not quite sticky. This dough is easiest to roll out if used soon after it's made, and a bit stiffer if refrigerated. Divide dough in half and roll out on floured board (arrowroot is great) to about 1/8" thickness. Transfer to pie pan and cut excess. Press edges down for 2-crust pies, double edge and pinch for 1-crust pie.

FOR CUSTARD, CREAM OR COOKED VEGETABLE PIE:
PUT CRUST IN PIE PAN, DOUBLE AND PINCH EDGES AND BAKE AT 400° 15-20 MIN. ADD FILLING AND ALLOW TO SET. THEN EAT.

TO PICK UP ROLLED CRUST, FOLD OVER ROLLING PIN AND TRANSFER TO PIE PAN.

FOR CRACKERS, ROLL OUT DIRECTLY ON COOKIE SHEET (GREASED), CUT OUT SHAPES, AND PICK OUT EXCESS DOUGH.

Goodies 185

BUTTER CRUST

1 c. butter (soft) or ghee
3 c. whole wheat pastry flour
1/4 t. salt if unsalted butter is used
boiling water

Blend flour, salt and butter together with fingers until it's blended evenly through flour
Add a bit of water at a time and work in until the dough is easy to work but not sticky. This one works best when chilled. Roll out and use like the basic crust.

COCONUT PIE CRUST   (uncooked)

1 1/2 c. raw or toasted coconut shredds
1/3 c. oil or butter (soft)
1 t. grated lime or lemon rind

Mix and press into pie pan. This is a no cook crust. Besides being good for custard pies and puddings, it's great filled with raw fresh fruits, berries or mixed plain, with honey or yoghurt.

ALMOND

NUT CRUST

3 c. ground nuts
1 c. soft butter, soy butter or oil
1/4 t. salt
1/4 c. honey (if sweet crust is wanted)

Mix together well and press 3/4 of it into pie pan. Add filling and sprinkle the remaining crust mixture on top. This need not be cooked.

GRANOLA CRUST

1/2 lb. granola
3/4 c. oil or 1 1/2 sticks butter (soft)

Mix together well and press into pan. Use uncooked or with cooked things like cheese cake.

APPLE-WALNUT PIE

basic pie crust recipe, doubled
6 lbs. apples, 24 med. size apples
3 c. (1 lb.) chopped walnuts
1 c. honey
1/2 c. oil

Mix ingredients well and pile high in 2 pie
pans lined with crust. Cover with solid top
crust and arrange a few extra walnuts on top.
Bake as in basic crust recipe.
Add 2 T. cinnamon to filling.

YAM-APPLE PIE

2 lbs. yams
3 lbs. apples
1/2 c. honey
double pie crust recipe
1/4 c. oil or butter

Slice yams and apples very thin. Mix with oil
and honey. Add 1 T. each allspice and cinnamon
if you like spice. Fill two pie shells and
cover with top shells. Bake as in basic crust
recipe for fruit pie.

STRAWBERRY PIE

3 pts. strawberries
1 c. water
1 c. honey
4 T., rounded, arrowroot starch (softened in
   cold water)
1 baked pie crust or 1 of the unbaked crusts

Wash and clean 1 pt. of strawberries. Add
honey and 4 rounded T. arrowroot starch to
water and berries. Bring to boil until thick.
Allow to cool. Wash and clean other 2 pts.
berries and put whole in crust. Pour semi-cool
liquid over berries and allow to set. Serve
with some whipped cream or soy cream with honey,
or eat it plain.

APPLES

CUT OUT CORE OF
APPLES AND SLICE
IN FAIRLY THIN
SLICES, NOT TOO
BIG.

AND LEAVE THE
SKINS WHERE THEY
BELONG
ON THE APPLE.

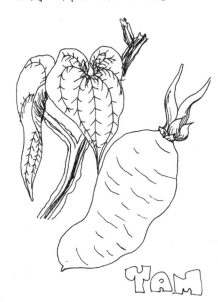

YAM

RAISIN-YOGHURT PIE

1 lb. thompson or manukka raisins
1 qt. yoghurt
1 c. boiling water
1/2 c. honey
juice of 2 lemons
1 nut or granola crust

Pour boiling water with honey dissolved in it
over raisins. Add lemon and yoghurt and set
aside. Prepare the crust and line a pie pan.
Put yoghurt-raisin mixture in and top with
another layer of crust. Bake in 400° oven for
25 min. Cool and serve.
Or: Mix yoghurt, raisins, honey and lemon together. Set over night like that in refrigerator. In the morning put it in one of the non-
cooked crusts and sprinkle a bit of the crust
on top. Chill together again, through the day.

ORANGE

ORANGE PIE

5-6 lbs. oranges
2 sticks kanten
1 c. water
1 pt. yoghurt
1 t. vanilla
1/2 c. honey
ground cashews
1 no-cook pie crust

Soak kanten in water for 15 min. Then, boil
slowly for another 15 min. and turn off heat.
Add honey, 1 1/2 qts. fresh squeezed orange
juice, rind of 1 orange, vanilla and stir. Let
it sit until somewhat cool and whip in yoghurt.
Put in pie shell and sprinkle generously with
nuts.
Use 1/2 c. tahini instead of the yoghurt or with
it.

COCONUT-ORANGE PIE

Follow the above recipe, adding 1 c. dry shredded coconut with the orange juice and other
things. Cool as above and add yoghurt. Slice
orange wedges and rings and decorate the top
with them.

LEMON PIE

8-10 lemons
1 c. arrowroot starch
1 1/2 qts. water
1 c. honey
1 no-cook pie crust or 1 cooked plain
2 c. soy butter

Soften arrowroot in 1/2 qt. of water. Bring
other qt. to a boil and add arrowroot to it.
When it has boiled and become thick and clear,
remove from heat. Add honey, fresh squeezed
lemon juice and rind from 3 lemons. Mix up,
cool a bit and pour into pie crust. Let set.
Whip up soy cream and serve on top or use real
whipped cream with honey.

TWO PUMPKIN PIES

1 med. pumpkin
1 c. soy butter
1 c. honey
2 T. cinnamon
1 T. allspice
1 t. nutmeg
2 t. coriander
2 c. nut milk or thick milk or yoghurt
1 t. vanilla
2 single crusts, plain

Remove seeds from pumpkin, wash, and set aside.
Cut up pumpkin into pieces (not too large) and
steam 20 min. in water. Puree through food
mill or sieve of some kind. Add honey, spices,
soy butter, milk and vanilla. Beat together,
pour into a shell and bake at 425° for 15 min.
and 350° for 30 min. (makes 2 pies)

PUMPKIN

PINEAPPLE-UPSIDE DOWN CAKE

1 fresh pineapple, peeled and sliced in 1/2"
  rounds with core removed
1 1/2 c. maple syrup
1 yellow cake recipe

Oil round baking pan or bowl and line with pineapple rings. Overlap if necessary. Pour 1/2 c.
maple syrup on slices. Make the yellow cake,
using maple syrup instead of honey. Pour batter
over pineapple and bake at 350° for 35-40 min.
Cool slightly and try to eat warm.

SORGHUM

GINGERBREAD

3 c. light flour
2 T. ground ginger or 4 T. fresh grated
1/2 c. oil or butter or 1 c. soy butter
4 eggs
1 t. baking soda
1/4 t. salt
1 c. sorghum or 1/2 c. honey and 1/2 c. black
  strap molasses
1 t. allspice
1 T. cinnamon
1/4 t. ground nutmeg
1 1/2 c. water
1 c. ground nuts

Mix honey, oil, egg yolks, salt, and spices until smooth. Mix soda and flour together and
add alternately with water to honey-oil mixture.
Beat until smooth and light. Add nuts and fold
in egg whites. Pour into oiled square bake pan
and bake at 350° for 40 min. Cool slightly and
cut. Eat warm, with whipped cream, butter.

SWEET POTATO PIE

2 lbs. sweet potatoes
1/2 c. soy butter
1 nut pie crust
1/2 c. maple syrup
1/2 c. thick cream or yoghurt

Boil sweet potatoes until tender. Cool enough
to peel. (Use peels in stock pot). Mash and
whip with syrup, soy butter and cream. Put in
pie shell and chill until set. (makes 1 pie)
If you like a thicker, sweeter pie, bake at
375° for 30 min. Cool until set.

CASHEW PIE

1 c. maple syrup
1 c. currants
1 lb. cashews
juice and rind of 1 lemon
1/2 lb. butter (1 c.) soft
1 c. cream
1 plain pie crust

Mix together chopped cashews, currants, maple
syrup, cream, butter and lemon. Put in shell
and bake at 425° 10 min., then 350° for 25-30
min.

CASHEWS

TAHINI CUSTARD PIE

1 c. tahini
3 c. water
1 t. vanilla
1 c. sorghum or honey
1 c. arrowroot flour
1 no-bake crust
1/2 c. carob powder

Bring 2 c. water to boil. Soften arrowroot in
1 c. cold water. Pour into boiling water and
stir until thick and clear. Add vanilla and
sorghum and cool slightly. Beat in tahini,
pour into pie shell and allow to set in cool
place.

STRAWBERRY-YOGHURT PIE

1 stick (agar-agar) kanten
2 c. water
1 c. honey
1 pt. strawberries, mashed
1 pt. yoghurt
1 cooked pie shell or 1 no-bake pie

Soak kanten in water for 15 min. Bring to boil and cook covered 20 min. Add honey and straw-berries. Set until semi-firm and whip in yo-ghurt. Pour into pie shell and allow to set.

SEA COLLANDERS

SOURCE OF AGAR-AGAR (KANTEN) GROWS FROM BERING SEA TO SAN JUAN IS., WASH MASS. TO ELLESMERE IS.

WILD STRAWBERRY FLOWER

CREAM PIE

3/4 c. honey
1/3 c. whole wheat pastry or other fine flour
1/4 t. salt
2 eggs
1 1/4 c. scalded cream or half milk
1 t. vanilla

Beat eggs and mix with flour and salt. Stir in honey and milk, mix together, a little at a time till all is added and smooth. Cook mix-ture in a pan of boiling water, stirring all the while, until mixture thickens. Cool and add vanilla. Will fill one sm. pie crust.
Cool until set.
If richer cream is wanted add 2 T. butter with vanilla.
Carob Cream: Add 1/2 c. carob powder mixed with flour.
Coffee-Mocha-Cream: Add 2 round T. pero and 1/2 c. carob to flour.
Coconut Cream: Add 1 c. shredded coconut to recipe with vanilla.
Banana: Add 3 diced bananas to cool filling and use juice of 1 lemon instead of vanilla.

CRANBERRY CUSTARD PIE

4 beaten eggs
2 1/2 c. honey
cinnamon
4 c. cranberries
1/4 t. salt
1/2 t. vanilla
1 c. milk, scalded

Put cranberries through food chopper or mince
with a knife. Add 1 c. honey and heat until
honey is blended with cranberries. Put in
pastry shell. Mix together eggs, 1/2 c. honey,
pour over cranberries and bake 450° for 10 min.
Turn down to 350° for 30-40 min. Let it cool
until set.

WILD STRAWBERRY

APPLE TURNOVERS

dough of plain crust recipe
1/2 c. butter or soy butter
3 lbs. apples
3/4-1 c. honey (some people like this with no
  honey)
1 t. cinnamon

Core and slice apples thin. Mix with honey and
cinnamon. Set aside. Roll out 1/2 of the double crust and spread some of butter on it.
Fold in half and roll out again. Butter, fold,
and roll again and again. Then divide into 3
pieces, roll to around 1/8" thick, a little
more. Spoon apple mixture into center of
round. Fold over and seal with your fingers.
Baste with oil, sprinkle with a little cinnamon, and bake at 375° for 30-40 min., until
brown and crispy. (makes 6 altogether)

CRANBERRY

APRICOT HATS

1 lb. dry, unsulphured apricots
2 c. water
1/2 c. honey (if you like it tart, don't use
  honey)
juice of 2 lemons
two crust pie dough recipe

Boil water, add honey and pour over apricots.
Allow to sit several hours or over night. Make
pie dough and divide into 12 pieces. Roll half
into 3" rounds. Mash up apricots and mix with
lemon. Spoon onto circles. Roll the other
half into a bit larger circles and cover apricots. Seal with fingers around edges. Bake
at 375° for 30-40 min. (6 hats)

APPLE BASKET COOKIES

Take 2 parts rolled oats to 1 part whole wheat.
Add a little salt, cinnamon, and oil. Mix with
hands until crumbly and moist. Add water until
you have a sticky pie type dough (apple juice
can be used instead of water). Cut up apples,
depends on how many cookies you want, 4 big
apples make about 12-15 lg. cookies. Cook apples, cinnamon and a bit of water with a couple
T. of arrowroot flour (starch) softened in it.
Stir until thickened. Take good size balls of
the dough and press into flat shapes with a
basket in the center. Spoon in apple mixture
and bake at 375° until browned and cooked
through, about 25 min.

CURRANT-CORNMEAL COOKIES

1 c. currants, soaked overnight in 1 c. apple
  juice
juice of 2 lemons
2 c. cornmeal
1 c. pastry flour
1/4 t. salt
3/4 c. oil

Mix everything together and spread into big
round cookies on oiled sheet. Bake at 400°
for 20-25 min. (makes about 1 doz. lg. cookies)

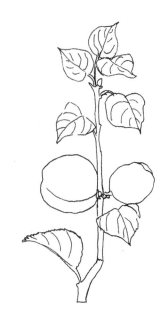

APRICOT

SUNFLOWER-RAISIN COOKIES

2 c. oatmeal
1 c. flour
1 c. honey
1/2 c. oil or 1 c. soy butter
1/4 t. salt
1 c. raisins soaked overnight in 1 c. water
1 c. sunflower seeds

Mix everything together in that order. Spread
out flat on oiled baking sheet and bake at
400-425° for 20-25 min., until golden.
(makes 12-18 cookies)

CARROT COOKIES

2 c. grated carrot (about 1 lb. carrots)
1/2 c. honey
1 c. chopped nuts
1 c. pastry flour
1/2 c. arrowroot flour
1/2 c. oil, plus 2 T.
1 t. cinnamon

Heat 2 T. oil and saute carrots 2-3 min., stirring lightly. Add to mixture of other ingredients. Drop into little round shapes on
greased cookie sheet and bake at 400° for 15-
20 min.

DATE PALM

FRUIT DROPS

1/2 c. cream
1/2 c. honey
1 t. vanilla
2 c. shredded coconut
1 c. chopped apricots, dates, prunes, mixed

Combine everything and drop an inch apart on
greased cookie sheet. Bake 12 min. at 350°,
until browned. (about 2 dozen cookies)

HONEY WAFERS

2 c. whole wheat pastry flour
1 c. butter (soft) or soy butter
2 c. honey
2 beaten eggs
1 c. ground or shredded almonds
1/4 t. nutmeg, 1/2 t. cinnamon (if you like spices)

Whip honey and butter together, add eggs. Mix in a combination of flour, spice and almonds. Drop small pieces onto greased cookie sheet (give them room) and bake at 300° for 12 min. Cool a min. and remove. Let them get crisp. Or: Roll around handle of a wooden spoon while still hot and allow to them to get crisp in a cylinder shape.

CREAM CHEESE COOKIES

1 c. whole wheat pastry flour
1/2 t. salt
1/2 c. soy butter or butter
1/4 lb. cream cheese
1/4 c. honey
1 T. caraway seeds

Whip soft butter and cream cheese together with caraway seeds. Then beat in honey and mix in flour and salt. Shape into a 2" roll and chill until solid, then slice thin. Bake at 400° for 6-10 min. (1 - 1 1/2 dozen)

BUTTER COOKIES

1 c. butter (unsalted), soft
3 c. flour (whole wheat pastry)
1/2 t. vanilla extract
1/8 t. salt
1 beaten egg (if wanted)
1 c. honey

PLUM

Mix together butter, honey, vanilla and egg. Add flour and salt and mix well. Chill and roll out between 1/8 and 1/4 inches thick. Cut into all your favorite shapes. Bake at 350° for 12 min., until golden. (makes nearly 2 dozen)

CREAM CHEESE-JELLY COOKIES

recipe for cream cheese cookies, doubled, omit
  caraway seeds
1/2-3/4 c. jelly or jam made with honey and no
  sugar
1/2 c. ground nuts

Make 2 rolls in 3" diameter. Cut roll into 10-
12 thin slices. On half the slices spoon some
jelly and sprinkle with ground nuts. In the
remaining rounds, cut out holes in the center,
about 1 " diameter. Cover other half with it
and seal edges. Bake on ungreased cookie sheet
at 400° for 10-15 min. Jelly will bubble up
through hole like a little spring.
(makes 5-6 big cookies)

PEANUT BUTTER COOKIES

1 c. peanut butter, made from peanuts only, and
  maybe some salt
3 c. whole wheat flour
1 c. honey
1/4 c. oil or butter
2 T. cream or yoghurt
2 beaten eggs (I've done this without eggs and
  it's okay)
1/4 t. salt (omit if salt is in peanut butter)

Mix together oil, honey, peanut butter, cream
and eggs. Beat until light and creamy. Beat
in salt and flour, a little at a time. Drop
by small spoonfuls onto greased cookie sheet.
Bake at 350° for 10-12 min., until brown.
(makes almost 2 1/2 dozen)

GRANOLA COOKIES

1 lb. granola (no sugar)
1 c. arrowroot flour
1/2 c. carob powder
1 c. soy butter or 1/2 c. oil
1 t. vanilla
a hit of cinnamon, nutmeg and allspice
1/2 c. honey (this cookie is real nice without honey, too)
1/2 c. dry currants or raisins, soaked in 1 c. water

Cream together honey, oil, vanilla, and spice. Add currants and water, carob, flour, and granola, in that order, and beat each in. Spoon little drops onto oiled cookie sheet and bake in 375° for 15 min., until browned lightly. (makes 2 1/2 - 3 dozen little cookies)

GRANOLA COOKIE CAKE

Make granola cookie recipe. Add 6 beaten egg yolks to oil (or 1 c. butter) and honey. Add remaining ingredients and just before baking, fold in 6 stiffly beaten egg whites. Pour into shallow lg. pan and bake at 350° for 20-25 min. Cool a bit and cut.

COCONUT MACAROONS

1 c. coconut shredds
1/2 c. honey
3 egg whites
1/4 t. salt

Mix honey and coconut together until smooth and add salt. Beat egg whites in one at a time until light and fluffy. Let stand 20 min. Drop little bits onto brown paper covered cookie sheet, ungreased. Bake at 300° for 30 min. or until dry on surface. Remove from paper when slightly cool. (almost 2 dozen macaroons)

BRAZIL NUTS

ALMOND MACS

1 c. almond butter
1/2 c. honey
1/4 t. salt
3 egg whites

Cook as you would with the coconut macaroons.

CAROB MACS

3/4 c. honey
1/2 t. vanilla
1/2 c. carob powder
1 c. almond butter or 1 c. coconut, shredded or
   mixed
3 egg whites

Follow the other macaroon recipes.

PEACH

HALF-CUP MACAROONS

1/2 lb. almond meal, freshly ground
1/2 c. honey
1/2 c. chopped dates
1/2 c. chopped dry pineapple (not sugar-dipped)
1/2 c. egg whites (about 4 eggs) stiffly beaten
   with 1/4 t. salt

Mix almond meal, honey and fruit. Fold in beat-
en egg whites and drop by little spoonfuls onto
ungreased sheet. Bake at 300° for 25 min.
(about 2 dozen little drops)

Neither of the two following ice cream recipes
need a special freezer.

LEMON ICE CREAM

2 c. cream or soy butter
3/4 c. honey
2 T. fresh lemon peel
1/3 c. lemon juice, fresh

Stir cream and honey until honey is dissolved.
Whip until stiff and thick. Add lemon peel and
lemon and freeze immediately.
(makes almost a pint and a half)

SNOW CREAM

I have saved my favorite for last. This one
only comes in winter when the fire inside is
warm and the night is bright by snowlight. Only
way to make this is with fresh fallen snow. Put
as much as you want in a big bowl. Then beat
in your favorite topping. For example:

thick cream, honey and vanilla
cream, honey, carob, vanilla
with chopped nuts
with nut milk instead of cream
with cinnamon
with sorghum instead of honey, or maple syrup
add pero to vanilla or carob

Blend any of the above ingredients together as
a topping. The best part of this is running
out with the bowl in your bare feet to get snow.
Sometimes it's so fine you even forget it's cold.

LEMON

15
BEVERAGES

Fresh vegetable and fruit juices of any kind are always good for you. Bottle juices are inferior in taste and nutrition to fresh juices because of pasteurization. This is a unique process which allows things to store infinitely, devoid of food value. If you like to drink a flavor rather than water, drink bottle juices. But it's only fair you know you aren't getting much food value.

UMEBOSHI PLUM JUICE

10 or so salted plums
1 qt. water

Boil together slowly, covered, for 20 min. Great hot or cold. Helps the body retain moisture and it quenches thirst beautifully.

LEMONADE HOT OR COLD

Bring 1 qt. or 1 c. water to boil. For every c. water add juice of 1 lemon and 2 T. honey.

ORANGE-MINT COOLER

To 1 c. mint tea add 2 T. honey. Chill. Squeeze juice from 2 oranges and add to tea. (makes 2 cups)

APPLE-MINT COOLER

Add 2 T. honey to 1 c. hot mint tea. Chill and mix with 1 c. fresh apple juice.

APPLE-TAHINI SHAKE

Put 2 c. apple juice (fresh) in qt. jar. Add 4 T. honey, 3 T. tahini and juice of 2 lemons and shake until foamy and well mixed.

ADUKI JUICE

Bring 2 T. aduki beans to a boil in 1 qt. water and bubble gently, covered until 1/2 the liquid is gone. Delicious alone or with a dash of tamari, a little lemon, some dill or savory.

PERRIER SODA

Mix 1/2 glass of perrier mineral water with 1/2
glass of your favorite fresh fruit juice.

SOY MILK WITH WHOLE BEANS

For this you need a couple yds. of cheese cloth,
a strainer, a blender, and 2 lg. pans. Wash
and soak 2 c. soy beans overnight in 2 qts.
water. Put soy beans, a little at a time, and
water in blender and turn on 10 seconds or so.
Lay cheesecloth, folded 4 thicknesses, in strainer and sit over pan. Pour soy liquid through.
Hold cheesecloth ends together to form a bag
and knead soy milk out with free hand. It's
easiest if you do a little at a time, then you
can milk it like a goat. Save soy solid for
making soybean pizza, like aduki pizza or soy
burgers or loaf. Heat liquid soy milk over
low flame and boil gently for 20 min. Stir
once in a while to keep from scorching. Drink
warm or cold. Some people like to sweeten soy
milk with honey, 2 T. to a c. This makes
2 qts. soy milk.

SOY MILK WITH SOY FLOUR

1 c. freshly ground soy flour (if you like,
   toast the flour until brown)
4 c. water

Add water to soy flour, a little at a time,
mixing until smooth with each addition. Bring
to low boil over low flame and cook for 20 min.,
stirring now and again. Cool. I usually don't
bother to strain this, but if you wish, pour
the milk into jar through cheesecloth layed in
a funnel. This, too, can be sweetened of
course.

SESAME MILK

This, too, has two ways of making. No. 1:

1 c. whole sesame seeds
1 qt. water

Whip in blender for several seconds, strain
through cheesecloth into qt jar. Honey makes
it sweeter.

No. 2:

1 c. tahini
1 qt. water

Pour cold water slowly into tahini, beating well
each time. Neither of these or any other nut
milks get cooked. Milk can be made from almonds, cashews, sunflower seeds. You name it,
from the whole nut or nut butter.
Save the nut solids to add in sweets, breads,
sauces.

GOLDEN MILK

This recipe comes from 3-Ho Foundation. Yogi
Bhajan says it will keep your joints lubricated.
I've seen it done many ways; this is the way I
do it:

1 c. milk
1 t. turmeric
1 T. oil (almond, preferably; my second choice
  and more common is sesame oil)
2-3 T. honey

Heat turmeric over low flame a few seconds.
Slowly add milk, stirring, and heat to drinking
temperature. Add honey and drink.

DATE MILK

Pour warm milk over dates and let sit in refrigerator a day. Warm and drink.

DANDELION

EVERY PART IS EDIBLE.

ROOT IS A TEA OR IS
ROASTED AS A
COFFEE SUBSTITUTE.

YOUNG LEAVES CAN
BE USED IN SALADS
OR COOKED. PICK
BEFORE FLOWERS
COME.

NUT-MILK-LASSE

1 c. milk
2 T. molasses
2 T. torula (plant) yeast

Shake it up. For B vitamins and protein, it's
a good thing.

MILK-LASSE

Made like nut-milk-lasse with dairy milk.

PERO

Pero is the name brand of a coffee substitute
made from roasted barley and rye. There are
many similar substitutes: pioneer with roasted
barley and chicory and figs, reform with barley
and chicory, bambu with barley, chicory, figs,
and acorns, dandelio with roasted dandelion
root, bardhan with roasted burdock root and
chicory and countless similar things. Except
for the last two, you just add water and mix;
it's in instant powder form. As for dandelio
and bardhan, they can be treated like coffee,
boiled very gently and strained, or perked or
any other method you have.

HOT CAROB

2 c. milk of any kind
1/2 c. carob powder
1/2 c. honey
1/2 t. vanilla

Add milk slowly to carob, mixing it smooth.
Heat slowly just to drinking warmth and add
honey and vanilla. Pour in cups.

MOCHA

Mix 1 c. hot pero with 1 c. hot carob and beat
together. Top with whipped cream. Good stuff!

THE YOUNG BUDS CAN
BE USED AS A RAW
OR COOKED VEGETABLE

AND OF COURSE THE
FLOWERS ARE FOR
THE TABLE, FOR WINE
AND FOR MAKING THE
FIELDS ALL YELLOW
IN SPRINGTIME.

DANDELIO-TAHINI FIZZ

Beat with a wire whip or in blender

1 c. dandelio tea
2 T. tahini
2 T. honey
1/2 t. vanilla
1 t. cinnamon

YOGHURT-BERRY SHAKE

1 c. yoghurt (8 oz.)
1/2 c. milk
1/4 c. honey
1 c. mashed, ripe strawberries, currants, blueberries, blackberries, rasberries, and on.
Beat by hand or in blender until smooth.

ORANGE SHAKE

1 c. orange juice
2 scoops vanilla ice cream or 1 c. rich milk,
  2 T. honey and 1/4 t. vanilla

Beat together and drink.

FRUIT JUICE SODA

Put 2 scoops of ice cream in a glass and pour
your favorite fruit juice over it. Or pour a
mixture of 3 T. fruit concentrate and 1/2 c.
perrier spring water over ice cream.

BLACKBERRY

ROASTED RICE AND GREEN TEA

Dry roast 2 T. rice until golden brown. Add
to 4 c. boiling pot of water and simmer gently
for 20 min. Remove from flame and add 4 spoons
bancha tea (japanese green tea) steep 10 min.
Serve with tamari. A bit of lemon is good, too.

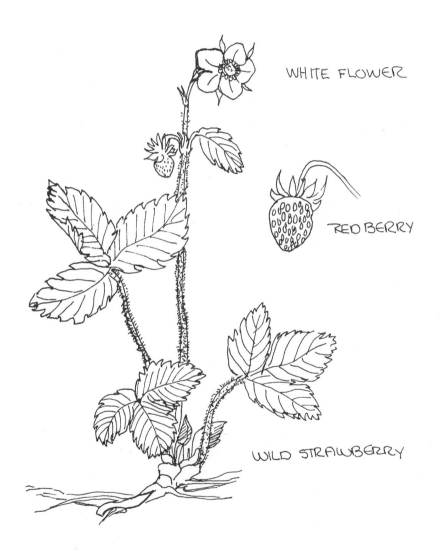

WHITE FLOWER

RED BERRY

WILD STRAWBERRY

HELPFUL INFORMATION

NEW OR UNFAMILIAR FOODS

In much of this book there are ingredients used
that still might not be familiar to everyone.
Don't let new foods frighten you. Most of the
time you've been using similiar foods and it's
just a matter of adjusting to unfamiliar flavors and names.

I like to use ingredients from all types of
cultures, diets, etc. I don't like to feel
limited. I let my intuition and taste guide
me. There really are no set rules! You can
experiment and see for yourself. Here's a list
of some foods and helpful information:

Tamari: I use this in almost everything. I
change off between the hearty, broth flavor of
tamari soy sauce as compared to the familiar
taste of salt. There is no other soy sauce
that can be substituted for tamari. There are
many soy sauces cheaper than tamari, but none
worth buying. Tamari is a fermented product
made from soy beans, water, whole wheat, and
sea salt aged together 18 months. It makes a
dark brown clear liquid which is a flavor help-
er and is a salting agent, too. Most of my
recipes call for tamari, but if you can't get
a hold of some, use 1 1/2 t. salt instead to
every 2 T. tamari.

Miso Soy Bean Paste: This is another fermented
soy product. It can be made from soy beans,
water and sea salt and aged in a barrel for 3
years. This is called hacho miso, the strong-
est one of all. A medium strength miso, a bit
on the light side is mugi miso. Made with soy-
beans, water, barley and sea salt. Kome miso,
the baby, is only a 2 year mild miso. Made
with soy beans, water, brown rice, and sea salt.
In all three, you have fine miso if the pieces
of the soy bean halves have remained fairly
whole. Pieces can be mashed into a paste in
a suribachi (Japanese grinding bowl) before
adding to recipes, or any method of smoothing
the paste can be used. Most of the time it is
done with a fork in a bowl.

Tahini: This is becoming a common food in
health food stores and even supermarkets. Tahini (tah-hee-nee) is hulled, crushed sesame
seeds, just a little thinner than peanut butter. When it is old, it thickens and becomes
dry. It still can easily be used in cooking
by thinning the thick tahini with warm water
before adding to sauces, salad dressings,
spreads, desserts, candies. An excellent protein source and a creamy texture add nutrition
and a milky thick consistency wherever tahini
is used.

Sesame butter: Made and used the same as tahini. The only difference is the whole sesame
seed is used for sesame butter giving it a
slightly stronger flavor than tahini. It is
also more nutritional with the unhulled seed.

Umeboshi (salted) Plum: One of the least known
foods I use. The salted plums are made by
packing japanese green plums, salt and chiso
leaves (to give the plums a pink color) in a
barrel for 3 years until salt has permeated
the plums. Umeboshi plums are used as a pre-
serving agent in pickles and prepared foods,
as a substitute for lemon in salad dressings,
and you can even make a juice from them.

Gomasio: A mixture of roasted, crushed sesame
seeds mixed with sea salt. The ratio is 5
parts seeds to 1 part salt or any proportions
you happen to prefer. I use 10 parts seeds to
1 salt. Refrigerate whatever is not consumed
immediately.

Oils: Stay away from bargain oils, especially
those oils made with cottonseed. Cottonseed
is not considered a food by the people who regu-
late the amount of poisons that can be used in
growing food. Check labels carefully. You can
usually get pure oil (Erewhon, Like It Was, and
Chico San are some dependable quality brands).
Planter's peanut oil isn't too bad, either.
Good oils make lighter, better tasting food.

Arrowroot Flour, Powder, or Starch: They are all from the white round arrowroot, cultivated mainly in the orient. Any of the three are interchangeable in any recipe calling for arrowroot. It is a thickener for puddings, pies, sauces, and a leavening agent for tempura batter, cakes, and pastries.

Kuzu: Sometimes confused with arrowroot. It should be understood that arrowroot is a thickener preferred to cornstarch because it is lighter and clearer. Kuzu is a medicine made from wild kuzu root, a native to Japan. It is a binding medicine and a perspirant, and not for everyday cooking.

Tekka: A dark, crumbly substance made with soy beans, salt and other root vegetables like burdock, carrot, or ginger until dark brown. It can be sprinkled on salads, grains, or vegetables and added to dressings and sauces for flavoring.

THE ORGANIC
DIRECTORY
$1.95
prepared by
RODALE PRESS
EMMAUS, PA. 18049

A DIRECTORY OF
ORGANIC FOOD SOURCES
LISTED BY STATE AND
INFORMATION ON
EARTH SAVING
WAYS OF LIVING.

ABBREVIATIONS & MEASUREMENTS

Abbreviations:

```
T.   = tablespoon
t.   = teaspoon
c.   = cup
min. = minute
hr.  = hour
oz.  = ounce
lb.  = pound
gal. = gallon
qt.  = quart
pt.  = pint
lg.  = large
med. = medium
sm.  = small
sim. = simmer
```

Liquids

```
1 tablespoon    = 1/2 oz.
3 teaspoons     = 1 tablespoon
1 cup           = 8 oz.
16 tablespoons  = 1 cup
2 cups          = 1 pint
2 pints         = 1 quart
4 quarts        = 1 gallon
```

Dry

```
1 pound         = 2-3 cups (it varies)
1 pound         = 16 oz.
16 tablespoons  = 1 c.
```

INDEX

217

73 74 75   12 11 10 9 8 7 6 5 4 3 2 1